GORDON RAMSAY'S

WORLD KITCHEN

KEY PORTER BOOKS

FOOD BY
GORDON RAMSAY
WITH MARK SARGEANT

TEXT BY
EMILY QUAH

PHOTOGRAPHS BY
CHRIS TERRY

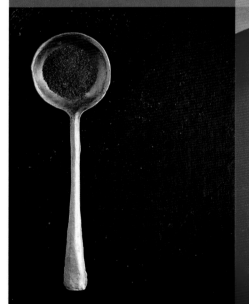

Introduction

Food has become a lot more innovative and exciting over the past decade or so. We are really spoilt for choice when it comes to restaurants offering enticing food from all corners of the globe. From exotic Thai curries to classic French fare, you are likely to find a variety of restaurants offering different styles of cooking in most towns and cities.

My work commitments over the past few years have taken me to lots of far-flung places, but every time I come home, I am continually impressed by the quality of food served at my favorite local restaurants. Like many of you, I love a good Friday-night curry. Granted, my local "curry house" boasts a Michelin star of its own, but I find that the food can be just as good as some of the dishes I sampled during my recent tour of India.

However, it's not all about Michelin stars. It is true that there are still restaurants serving inferior food, but fortunately for everyone, the credit crisis has forced restaurants to re-evaluate their business and deliver value to their customers. This not only means offering consistent good food at reasonable prices, but also a good ambience, friendly, and attentive service, and general cleanliness. It's all common sense stuff that has somehow evaded the conscience of many a restaurant manager until now.

Another positive "side effect" of the financial crisis is that entertaining at home is on the up. I'm hoping that as a consequence, we are cooking more. And as our palates adapt and evolve, so too should our cooking repertoire. The variety of exotic ingredients now available at most supermarkets has made it easy and convenient for us to cook a wide range of dishes, from an Italian osso buco to Middle Eastern dolmades. Any ingredient that is not found at a major grocery chain may require a trip to an Asian or Middle Eastern food store, but think of these sorties less as an inconvenience and more a route to discovery. After all, the best way to learn about unusual ingredients is by cooking them.

For this book, I've chosen a selection of my favorite dishes from ten very different cuisines—from the best cuisines in Europe to those from China, Thailand, and other faraway lands. Each cuisine is tied to a culture steeped in tradition and local custom, so my limited selection of recipes can only be a taster to whet the appetite. The recipes are also my take on these dishes, often with a little innovative twist to make them more accessible and easy to cook at home. I hope that they will inspire you to step out of your comfort zone and try something new every week. Enjoy ...

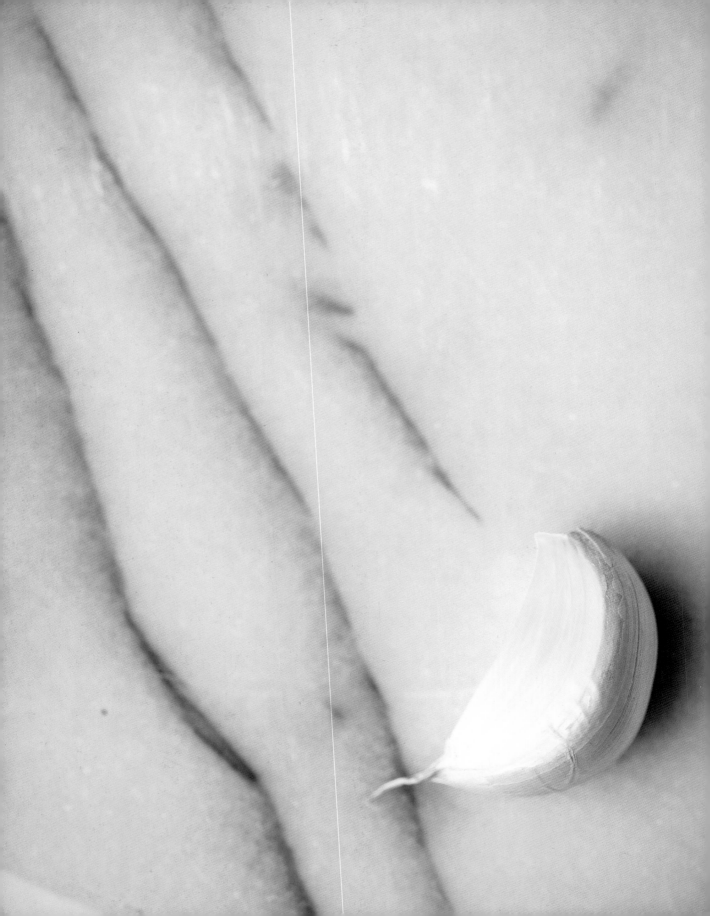

FRENCH

ALTHOUGH MY FOOD HAS CHANGED AND NOW HAS A
MORE ECLECTIC STYLE, MY HEART STILL BELONGS TO
FRANCE. MY FORMATIVE YEARS WERE SPENT TRAINING
WITH THE ROUX BROTHERS AND A THREE-YEAR STINT
IN PARIS TAUGHT ME A GREAT DEAL ABOUT FRENCH
CUISINE. WHENEVER I RETURN, I GO TO THE MARKETS
—THE AMAZING PRODUCE NEVER CEASES TO INSPIRE
ME AND I'M BUZZING WITH IDEAS WHEN I GET BACK
HOME. THERE ARE SO MANY FANTASTIC DISHES AND,
OF COURSE, THERE'S THE WINE! OVER THE YEARS,
WE HAVE LEARNED A LOT FROM FRENCH COOKING AND
WE SHOULD NEVER FORGET THAT. YES, THINGS HAVE
MOVED ON DRAMATICALLY, BUT WITHOUT AUGUSTE
ESCOFFIER OR FERNAND POINT WHERE WOULD WE BE?

Brandade on garlic toasts

THIS IS MY TAKE ON THE CLASSIC brandade. Instead of salted cod, which calls for lengthy soaking, I gently poach fresh cod in olive oil to achieve a tender and succulent result. For a delicious appetizer, serve the brandade and garlic toasts with a lightly dressed mixed salad and chilled crisp, dry white wine.

SERVES 6–8

Brandade:

10oz (300g) cod fillet, skinned
$^2/_3$ cup (150ml) olive oil
$^1/_2$ tsp (2ml) rock salt
2 thyme sprigs
$^3/_4$lb (350g) potatoes, such as
   Russet
$^2/_3$ cup (150ml) heavy cream
$^2/_3$ cup (150ml) whole milk
2 garlic cloves, peeled and sliced
sea salt and black pepper
2 basil sprigs, leaves shredded

Garlic toasts:

4–6 small baguettes
   (or 1–2 large ones)
1 large garlic clove, peeled and
   halved
extra-virgin olive oil, to drizzle

Check the fish for small bones, removing any with kitchen tweezers. Place the cod, olive oil, rock salt, and a thyme sprig in a small saucepan. Place the pan over the lowest possible heat and cook very gently for 8 to 10 minutes until the fish begins to flake easily. Let cool, then drain well, saving the oil. Flake into large pieces.

Peel the potatoes and cut into $^3/_4$-inch (2cm) cubes. Place in a saucepan with the cream, milk, garlic, remaining thyme sprig, and some seasoning. Simmer for 10 to 12 minutes until soft. Drain, discarding the thyme, then mash lightly. Mix with the flaked cod, adding some of the reserved oil, and season with salt and pepper to taste. Allow to cool, then stir in the shredded basil leaves. The brandade is best served at room temperature.

When just about ready to serve, preheat the broiler to high. Thinly slice the baguettes on the diagonal (or halve small ones, if you prefer) and lay them on a baking sheet. Broil for about 1 minute (rounded sides up if halved) until lightly golden, then turn them over and rub the nontoasted sides with the garlic. Drizzle with extra-virgin olive oil and broil until golden and crisp. Don't leave unattended as the toasts can burn easily.

Spoon the brandade into small serving bowls and grind over some pepper. Place the garlic toasts alongside for everyone to help themselves at the table. Or serve the toasts topped with the brandade, if you prefer.

Moules marinière

ROPE-GROWN MUSSELS are now widely available pretty much all year round, which means that we can enjoy this lovely dish any time. It is equally suited to warm and chilly days. Serve in deep soup bowls with homemade fries if you like, plus mayonnaise and lots of crusty bread to mop up the flavorful juices.

SERVES 4

2lb (1kg) live mussels
1 onion, peeled and minced
1 shallot, peeled and minced
1 garlic clove, peeled and minced
1 bay leaf
3 thyme sprigs
handful of Italian parsley, stalks separated,
   leaves chopped
generous 3/4 cup (200ml) dry white wine
black pepper

Scrub the mussels clean under cold running water, scraping off any barnacles with a knife and tugging away any beards. Check over the mussels, discarding any that are cracked or open and do not close when sharply tapped. Rinse well and set aside.

Place the onion, shallot, garlic, bay leaf, thyme, parsley stalks, and wine in a large pan. Bring to a boil, then tip in the mussels and cover the pan with a tight-fitting lid. Give the pan one or two shakes, then let the mussels steam for 3 to 4 minutes until they have opened. Discard any that remain closed. Season with a good grinding of pepper. Mussels are naturally salty so you probably won't need to add salt.

Divide the mussels and cooking juices between warm large bowls and sprinkle with the chopped parsley. Serve immediately, remembering to provide bowls for the discarded empty shells.

Pan-frying scallops

Sweet, juicy, fresh scallops need to be treated with respect to retain their lovely succulence—overcook them and they turn horribly tough and rubbery. I use this simple technique to ensure quick, even cooking.

Cut the scallops in half horizontally into discs. Heat a thin film of olive oil in a heavy skillet until really hot. Season the scallops with sea salt and black pepper and lay them in the skillet, clockwise fashion in a circle. Pan-fry for 1 minute until golden at the edges, then turn them in the same order that you placed them in the skillet. Cook for no longer than a minute on the other side—the scallops should feel quite bouncy when lightly pressed. Squeeze over a little lemon juice and serve at once.

Pan-fried scallops with leeks vinaigrette

TENDER LEEKS AND VERY FRESH SCALLOPS both have a delightful natural sweetness and are perfect partners. A tangy mustardy vinaigrette provides a welcome contrast for this dish.

SERVES 4

12 large scallops, cleaned
2 tbsp (30ml) olive oil
sea salt and black pepper
squeeze of lemon juice

Leeks vinaigrette:
8 medium leeks, white part only, trimmed
1/2 cup (125ml) extra-virgin olive oil
1 tbsp (15ml) Dijon mustard
1 tbsp (15ml) cider or white wine vinegar
pinch of superfine sugar (optional)

To finish:
Italian parsley leaves

Set the cleaned scallops aside at room temperature while you prepare the leeks vinaigrette.

Thinly slice the white leeks, then wash thoroughly, drain, and pat dry. Heat 2 tbsp (30ml) extra-virgin olive oil in a wide sauté pan over medium heat and add the leeks with some seasoning. Sweat them, stirring occasionally, for 6 to 8 minutes until they are soft but not colored.

Meanwhile, make the vinaigrette. Put the remaining extra-virgin olive oil, mustard, vinegar, and a pinch each of salt and pepper into a screw-topped jar. Seal and shake well, then taste and adjust the seasoning, adding a pinch of sugar if necessary.

When the leeks are soft, add a few tablespoonfuls of the vinaigrette to the pan and toss until the leeks are nicely coated.

Now heat the olive oil in a wide skillet and pan-fry the scallops following my guide (on the preceding pages).

Spoon the leeks vinaigrette onto warm plates. Arrange the scallops on top and drizzle a little more vinaigrette around the plate (keep any remaining dressing in the refrigerator and use to drizzle over salads). Garnish the scallops with parsley leaves and serve immediately.

Tuna provençale

I ADORE THE FLAVORS OF PROVENCE, particularly the abundant use of fresh vegetables and herbs in many classic dishes. This healthy tuna and Mediterranean vegetable bake is light and flavorful, but you do need to get very fresh tuna especially if—like me—you prefer the fish on the rare side.

SERVES 4

4 fresh line-caught tuna steaks, about 6¹/₂oz (180g) each and ³/₄ inch (2cm) thick
2–3 tbsp (30–45ml) olive oil, plus extra to drizzle
1 red onion, peeled and chopped
4 garlic cloves, peeled and minced
1 sweet yellow pepper, cored, seeded, and chopped
1 sweet red pepper, cored, seeded, and chopped
sea salt and black pepper
2 medium zucchini, trimmed and roughly chopped
14oz (400g) can chopped plum tomatoes
1 thyme sprig
1 rosemary sprig
scant ¹/₂ cup (50g) pitted black olives
1 lemon, thinly sliced
handful of basil leaves, shredded (optional)

Preheat the oven to 400°F (200°C). Trim the tuna steaks if necessary and set aside.

Heat the olive oil in a wide pan. Add the onion, garlic, and peppers with some seasoning and sauté over medium-high heat for 5 to 6 minutes until they begin to soften but not color. Add the zucchini, stir well, and cook for another 2 to 3 minutes. Now add the chopped tomatoes, thyme, rosemary, and olives, mix well, and bring to a simmer. Cook for a few minutes, then transfer to a wide ovenproof dish.

Rub the tuna steaks all over with salt, pepper, and a little drizzle of olive oil. Overlap the tuna steaks on top of the vegetables and tuck the lemon slices in between. Add a generous grinding of pepper then place in the oven. Bake for about 8 to 10 minutes until the tuna is cooked to medium rare—the steaks should feel slightly springy when pressed. If you prefer tuna well done, bake for another 5 to 10 minutes until they feel just firm.

Scatter shredded basil over the dish, if you like, and serve straightaway. Delicious simply with good country bread, or with sautéed potatoes.

Confit duck leg
with sautéed potatoes

THIS TRADITIONAL DISH IS FROM PÉRIGORD, a region famed for its duck and goose foie gras. There, succulent and tender duck confit is customarily served with a salad and potatoes—either sautéed in the same flavorful fat in which the duck was cooked, or in a hearty gratin. A scrumptious, rich dish for the occasional indulgent meal.

SERVES 4

Confit duck legs:
4 duck legs
rock salt
handful of thyme sprigs
3 garlic cloves, peeled and sliced
2 bay leaves
2 x 12oz (350g) cans duck or
    goose fat

Sautéed potatoes:
1lb (500g) small waxy potatoes,
    such as Yukin Gold, peeled and
    halved
1 rosemary sprig, leaves minced
sea salt and black pepper

Sprinkle the duck legs all over with rock salt and let stand at room temperature for an hour.

Preheat the oven to 275°F (140°C). Rinse off the salt from the duck and pat dry with paper towels. Place the duck legs in a roasting pan in which they fit quite snugly and add the thyme, garlic, and bay leaves. Melt the duck fat in a saucepan over low heat. When it is translucent, carefully pour it over the duck legs, to cover them completely.

Cover the pan with foil and carefully place in the oven. Cook slowly for about 2 hours until the meat is very tender, making sure the legs remain covered by the fat. The duck is ready when the meat slips easily away from the bone. Remove from the oven.

Turn the oven setting up to 400°F (200°C). Lift the cooked duck legs out of the fat and place skin-side down in a roasting pan; reserve the fat. Roast the duck legs in the hot oven for 15 to 20 minutes, turning halfway. The skin will crisp up beautifully, while the meat remains tender.

Meanwhile, parboil the potatoes in a saucepan of boiling salted water for 4 to 5 minutes until half-cooked. Tip into a colander to drain and leave for a few minutes to dry off; this will help them to crispen. Place a nonstick skillet over medium-high heat and add a thin layer of the saved duck fat. When hot, add the potatoes with the rosemary and season well. Cook until the underside is golden brown, then turn and sauté for a few minutes until the potatoes are nicely colored and crisp all over, yet fluffy inside.

Serve the confit duck legs with the sautéed potatoes. Accompany with some grainy mustard and green beans, if you like.

Guinea fowl braised in cider with caramelized apples

THE NORMANDY REGION BOASTS SUPERB PRODUCTS, including wonderful cream, butter, apples, and Calvados—all of which are ingredients for the classic *poulet à la Normande*. For a change, I've replaced the chicken with guinea fowl, which I find to be more flavorful and well suited to the rich and creamy sauce. If guinea fowl is not available to you, by all means substitute with chicken.

SERVES 4

2 guinea fowl, about 1³/₄lb (800g) each, jointed
sea salt and black pepper
2–3 tbsp (30–45ml) olive oil
2 thin slices lean bacon, chopped
1¹/₄ cups (300ml) medium cider
generous ¹/₃ cup (100ml) Calvados or brandy
generous 1 cup (250ml) heavy cream
few thyme sprigs, leaves stripped
1lb (500g) firm, tart apples (about 3)
2 tbsp (30ml) butter
1–2 tsp (2–10ml) superfine sugar
squeeze of lemon juice, to taste
¹/₄ cup (30g) walnuts, toasted and lightly crushed
handful of Italian parsley, leaves chopped

Preheat the oven to 400°F (200°C). Season the guinea fowl joints with salt and pepper. Heat a thin layer of olive oil in a wide ovenproof casserole until hot. Brown the guinea fowl in batches for 2 to 3 minutes on each side until evenly colored, removing the pieces to a plate when they are ready.

Add the bacon to the casserole and pan-fry until lightly golden brown. Pour in the cider and Calvados, bring to a boil, and let bubble until reduced by one-third. Stir in the cream and thyme leaves.

Return the guinea fowl pieces to the casserole, put the lid on, and place in the oven. Braise for 30 to 45 minutes until the guinea fowl is tender and just cooked through; remove the breast pieces after 20 to 25 minutes to avoid overcooking and return them for the last 5 minutes to warm through.

About 15 minutes before you will be ready to serve the guinea fowl, peel, core, and thickly slice the apples into rings. Melt the butter in a large skillet. Sprinkle the apple slices with sugar and pan-fry them in the butter for about 4 to 5 minutes on each side until golden brown.

When the guinea fowl is ready, remove the pieces to a warm plate. If you find the sauce too thin, boil it until reduced and thickened to the desired consistency. Season to taste with salt, pepper, and a little lemon juice.

Return the guinea fowl to the sauce and garnish with the caramelized apples. Sprinkle the walnuts and chopped parsley on top before serving.

Navarin of lamb with spring vegetables

THIS ELEGANT DISH IS AN EASTER SPECIALTY in France. Tender braised lamb neck tenderloin and a medley of spring vegetables are brought together in a flavorful, light sauce. The dish does take a little time to make, but it certainly isn't difficult. It is important to brown the meat well and to use good-quality lamb stock.

SERVES 4

16 baby turnips, trimmed
16 baby carrots, peeled or
　scrubbed
16 baby leeks, trimmed
scant 1 cup (100g) peas, thawed
　if frozen
1 cup (120g) fava beans, skinned
12 pearl onions or small shallots,
　peeled
sea salt and black pepper
1³/₄lb (800g) lamb neck tenderloin
2¹/₂ tbsp (20ml) all-purpose flour,
　to dust
2 tbsp (30ml) olive oil
1¹/₄ cups (300ml) light red wine,
　such as Beaujolais
2 garlic cloves, peeled and
　chopped
1 bay leaf
3 thyme sprigs
3 rosemary sprigs
1³/₄ cups (400ml) chicken stock
3¹/₂ tbsp (50ml) cold butter, cut
　into small pieces
1 tbsp (15ml) superfine sugar
2 tbsp (30ml) balsamic vinegar
small handful of tarragon,
　leaves picked

For the vegetables, have a bowl of ice water ready and bring a large pan of salted water to a boil. Working in batches, blanch the turnips for 3 minutes, then remove to the ice water with a slotted spoon to refresh. Once cooled, scoop them out onto a plate. Repeat the process with the rest of the vegetables, blanching the carrots for 4 minutes, the leeks for 5 minutes, the peas and fava beans for 1 minute and, finally, the pearl onions for 8 to 10 minutes.

Cut the lamb into 1¹/₄-inch (3cm) chunks, dust with flour, and season with salt and pepper. Heat the olive oil in an ovenproof casserole or wide, heavy pan and cook the lamb, in batches if necessary, until browned all over. Tip the meat into a colander set over a bowl to catch the juices.

Place the casserole back on the heat and add the wine, garlic, bay leaf, thyme, and rosemary. Boil vigorously until reduced to a sticky syrup, then pour in the stock. Return the lamb to the casserole, along with any meat juices from the bowl. Bring to a simmer and skim off excess fat. Turn the heat right down and simmer very gently for about 2 hours, skimming every so often.

When the lamb is tender, remove the meat to a plate with a slotted spoon. Increase the heat and reduce the sauce down to a light coating consistency. Now whisk in the butter, a piece at a time. Season well with salt and pepper to taste, adding a little sugar and balsamic vinegar for a little sweetness and acidity if you like.

Return the lamb to the sauce and stir in the blanched vegetables. Bring to a simmer and reheat gently for 4 to 5 minutes. Divide between warm shallow bowls and scatter over the tarragon leaves. Serve at once.

Lemon **soufflé**

IT IS REALLY NOT THAT TRICKY TO MAKE A SOUFFLÉ and I'm determined to prove it! Those of you who shy away from them, please give this recipe a go. The secret lies in making a thick soufflé base and adequately whisking the egg whites until they are firm and glossy. Also, it is important to resist opening the oven door until the soufflé is ready, otherwise it is liable to collapse.

SERVES 4

3 tbsp (40ml) unsalted butter, well softened, for brushing
1/2 cup (100g) superfine sugar, plus extra to dust
2/3 cup (150ml) whole milk
generous 1/3 cup (100ml) heavy cream
3 large egg yolks
1 tbsp (15ml) all-purpose flour
1 1/4 tbsp (10ml) cornstarch
4 large egg whites
finely grated zest and juice of 2 lemons
confectioners' sugar, to dust

Brush 4 individual soufflé dishes (generous 1-cup/250ml capacity) with the softened butter, using upward vertical strokes, including the rims. Chill for a few minutes, then brush with a second layer of butter. Sprinkle some superfine sugar into each dish, shaking and tipping the dish to dust the base and sides evenly. Tip out any excess and chill until needed.

For the soufflé base, pour the milk and cream into a heavy pan and slowly bring to just below a boil, then remove from the heat. Meanwhile, whisk the egg yolks and 1/4 cup (50g) superfine sugar together in a large bowl until pale and thick. Sift the flour and cornstarch together onto the yolk mixture and whisk again until smooth. Now, slowly add the creamy milk, whisking as you go. Pour the mixture back into the pan and stir constantly over low heat with a wooden spoon for 5 minutes or so, until it is smooth and quite thick. Set aside to cool. Preheat the oven to 400°F (200°C).

In a large clean bowl, whisk the egg whites to stiff peaks. Add a few drops of lemon juice, then whisk again. Gradually whisk in the remaining 1/4 cup (50g) sugar, a spoonful at a time, until you have a thick, glossy mixture.

Stir the lemon zest and juice into the soufflé base, then whisk in a third of the egg white mix to loosen the mixture. Now carefully fold in the rest of the egg white, using a large metal spoon, until evenly incorporated.

Spoon the mixture into the prepared dishes, filling them to the top, then tap each once on the counter to get rid of any air bubbles. Gently smooth the surface with a small palette knife. Run the tip of the palette knife around the inside edge of the dish, then place on a baking sheet. Bake in the middle of the oven for 15 to 18 minutes or until risen with a slight wobble in the middle. Dust with confectioners' sugar and serve.

Chocolate crêpes with Chantilly cream

THIN CRÊPES ARE A SPECIALTY OF BRITTANY. Originally crêpes were always savory, made with locally milled buckwheat flour, but sweet ones have gained popularity over the years. My cream-filled chocolate version, drizzled with chocolate sauce, is satisfyingly rich. If you don't have a crêpe pan, just use a wide nonstick skillet.

SERVES 6–8

Crêpes:
- 3/4 cup (100g) all-purpose flour
- 1/4 cup (25g) cocoa powder
- 1/4 tsp (1ml) fine sea salt
- 1 tbsp (15ml) superfine sugar
- 2 medium eggs, lightly beaten
- 1 tbsp (15ml) melted butter, plus a few pieces for cooking
- 1 1/4 cups (300ml) whole milk
- 1 tsp (5ml) vanilla extract

Chocolate sauce:
- 3 1/2 oz (100g) good-quality dark chocolate (70% cocoa solids)
- 1 tbsp (15ml) unsalted butter
- 4 tsp (20ml) clear honey
- scant 5 tbsp (70ml) whole milk

Crème chantilly:
- 1 cup (250ml) heavy cream
- 2–3 tbsp (30–45ml) confectioners' sugar
- 1 tsp (5ml) vanilla extract

To serve:
- 4 tbsp (60ml) slivered almonds, lightly toasted
- candied orange zest (see page 102), optional

For the crêpes, sift the flour, cocoa powder, and salt into a bowl and stir in the sugar. Make a well in the center and tip in the beaten eggs, melted butter, milk, and vanilla extract. Whisk to combine the ingredients and form a smooth batter, but try not to overwork the mixture. Let stand or chill for at least 30 minutes.

For the chocolate sauce, break the chocolate into small pieces and place in a heatproof bowl over a pan of simmering water. Add the butter and honey and allow to melt, stirring from time to time. Remove from the heat and gradually whisk in the milk until you have a smooth sauce. If necessary, warm the sauce slightly before serving.

For the crème chantilly, in a bowl, whip the cream with the confectioners' sugar and vanilla to soft peaks. Cover and chill until ready to serve.

To cook the crêpes, place a nonstick crêpe pan over medium heat and add a piece of butter. When melted, tilt the pan so that the butter coats the bottom. Add a small ladleful of batter and swirl to evenly coat the bottom of the pan in a thin layer. Cook for about 1 1/2 minutes until the batter is set and golden brown underneath. Flip over to cook the other side for a minute. Transfer to a warm plate and wrap in a dish towel to keep warm. Repeat with the rest of the batter, stacking the crêpes interleaved with waxed paper in the dish towel as they are cooked.

To serve, spread a layer of crème chantilly over one half of each crêpe, scatter with a few toasted almonds. Fold the plain half of the crêpe over the filling to enclose, then fold again into quarters. Place one filled crêpe on each serving plate and drizzle over the chocolate sauce. Scatter over a few toasted almonds, and if you wish, top with some candied orange zest.

Raspberry tart

EXQUISITE PASTRIES AND TARTS IN PATISSERIES and bakeries across France never fail to seduce passersby. I'm always reminded of them by this irresistible, glistening *tarte aux framboise*. You will have more pie dough and possibly more vanilla cream than you need (it isn't practical to make a smaller amount), but you can always make some little tartlets.

SERVES 8–10

Sweet tart pie dough:
1/2 cup (125g) unsalted butter, softened to room temperature
scant 1/2 cup (90g) superfine sugar
1 large egg
generous 1 3/4 cups (250g) all-purpose flour, plus extra to dust
1 tbsp (15ml) ice-cold water (if needed)

Vanilla cream:
generous 1 cup (250ml) whole milk
1/2 vanilla bean, slit lengthwise and seeds scraped out
1/4 cup (50g) superfine sugar
2 1/2 tbsp (20ml) cornstarch
3 large egg yolks
generous 1/3 cup (100ml) heavy cream

Topping:
about 1 1/2lb (700g) raspberries, wiped (rather than washed)
2–3 tbsp (30–45ml) seedless raspberry jam, to glaze
1 tbsp (15ml) hot water (if needed)

To make the pie dough, whiz the butter and sugar in a food processor until just combined. Add the egg and whiz for 30 seconds. Tip in the flour and process for a few seconds until the dough just comes together, adding a little water if needed. Knead lightly on a floured counter. Shape into a disk, wrap in plastic wrap, and chill for 30 minutes.

Roll out the dough on a lightly floured counter to the thickness of 1/8 inch (3mm). Use it to line a 9–10-inch (23–25cm) tart pan with removable base, trimming off excess dough around the edges. Chill for at least 30 minutes.

For the vanilla cream, put the milk, vanilla seeds, and bean in a pan with 1 tbsp (15ml) of the sugar. Heat slowly until almost boiling. Meanwhile, beat the remaining sugar, cornstarch, and egg yolks together in a bowl. As the milk begins to scald, slowly trickle it onto the egg mix, stirring. Rinse out the pan. Pass the mixture through a strainer into the pan. Stir over low heat until it forms a thick custard. Pass through a strainer into a clean bowl and let cool, stirring occasionally, to prevent a skin forming.

Preheat the oven to 400°F (200°C) with a baking sheet inside. Line the pastry shell with waxed paper and dried beans. Place the tart pan on the baking sheet and bake for 15 to 20 minutes. Remove the paper and beans and return to the oven for 5 minutes to finish cooking the base. Let cool for 10 minutes, then unmold and cool on a wire rack.

Whip the cream to soft peaks. Beat the cooled vanilla custard slightly to loosen it, then fold in the cream. Chill until ready to serve. Spread a thin layer of vanilla cream in the pastry shell. Arrange the raspberries on top. Warm the raspberry jam a little, thinning it with the hot water if necessary, then brush over the berries to glaze. Best eaten slightly chilled on the day.

ITALIAN

I AM LUCKY ENOUGH TO HAVE WORKED A LOT IN ITALY,
PARTICULARLY IN TUSCANY AND SARDINIA. ITALIANS
ARE VERY PROUD AND PASSIONATE ABOUT THEIR
INGREDIENTS AND FOOD. ALMOST EVERY TOWN AND
VILLAGE HAS ITS OWN PASTA AND EACH ONE IS MADE
SPECIFICALLY FOR THE SAUCE IT IS SUPPOSED TO GO
WITH. THEY ALSO HAVE DEFINITE VIEWS ABOUT HOW
THEIR FOOD SHOULD BE EATEN. SHOULD YOU MAKE THE
MISTAKE OF ASKING FOR PARMESAN WITH A PASTA DISH
CONTAINING FISH, YOU'LL BE TOLD IN NO UNCERTAIN
TERMS THAT IT IS NOT THE DONE THING. TO ITALIANS,
FOOD IS SOMETHING THAT YOU GROW UP WITH AND AN
IMPORTANT PART OF LIFE, NOT JUST SOMETHING TO
KEEP YOU ALIVE. GOOD COOKING IS IN THEIR BLOOD.

Griddled zucchini
with prosciutto

PERFECT AS A SUMMER APPETIZER, or as part of an antipasto spread, this lovely dish is incredibly easy to make. You do, however, need to use very fresh zucchini and a good-quality cured ham—ideally prosciutto di San Daniele.

SERVES 4

4 large zucchini, trimmed
2 tbsp (30ml) olive oil
sea salt and black pepper
7oz (200g) good-quality prosciutto, thinly sliced
2 tbsp (30ml) pine nuts, toasted
handful of Italian parsley, leaves picked

Sweet and sour dressing:
2 tbsp (30ml) red wine vinegar
1–2 tbsp (15–30ml) blossom honey
juice of $\frac{1}{2}$ lemon
6 tbsp (90ml) extra-virgin olive oil
few thyme sprigs, leaves picked

First, make the sweet and sour dressing. In a small bowl, whisk together the wine vinegar, 1 tbsp (15ml) honey, and most of the lemon juice to combine, then gradually whisk in the extra-virgin olive oil. Stir in the thyme leaves and season with salt and pepper. Taste for seasoning, adding more honey or lemon if you feel it is needed. The dressing should have the perfect balance of sweet, salty, and sour.

Cut the zucchini on the diagonal into $\frac{1}{2}$ inch (1cm) thick slices. Tip them into a large bowl, add the olive oil, salt and pepper, and toss well to coat. Heat up a griddle pan over medium-high heat, then cook the zucchini slices for 3 to 4 minutes on each side until they are lightly browned and tender.

Arrange the slices of prosciutto and zucchini on individual plates. Drizzle over the sweet and sour dressing and scatter over the pine nuts and parsley leaves. Serve warm or at room temperature.

Wild mushrooms on griddled polenta with pecorino

THIS IS THE ITALIAN ANSWER to our mushrooms on toast. Griddled polenta is a brilliant base for sautéed flavorful mushrooms and when served as a generous portion, it is substantial enough for a lunch with a leafy salad on the side. Do use a good mix of wild mushrooms when in season. At other times of the year, buy a selection of portabello, oyster, and brown crimini mushrooms.

SERVES 4

1^1/$_3$ cups (200g) instant polenta
5 cups (1.2 liters) water
sea salt and black pepper
2 tbsp (30ml) olive oil, plus extra
    for brushing
1lb (500g) mixed wild mushrooms,
    cleaned
4 garlic cloves, peeled and
    chopped
2 tbsp (25ml) butter
few oregano sprigs, leaves
    picked
2–3 tbsp (30–45ml) all-purpose
    flour, to dust
pecorino shavings, to garnish

First, prepare the polenta. Pour the water into a medium saucepan, salt lightly, and bring to a boil. Add the polenta gradually in a thin, steady stream, whisking constantly. Keep stirring for about 5 minutes until the polenta thickens and all the water has been absorbed. When ready, remove from the heat, season well with salt and pepper, and tip onto a lightly oiled baking tray. Using a palette knife, spread the polenta evenly, to a ^{3}/$_4$ inch (2cm) thickness. Let cool and set for 30 minutes.

When you are just about ready to serve, halve any larger mushrooms. Place a large skillet over high heat. When hot, add the olive oil followed by the mushrooms and cook quickly until they begin to color. Stir in the garlic and butter with some seasoning and half the oregano leaves. Continue to cook the mushrooms over high heat until any liquid released has been cooked off. Take the skillet off the heat; keep warm.

Put a griddle pan over medium heat. Cut the polenta into 3^1/$_4$–4-inch (8–10cm) squares and dust with a little flour, then brush the griddle with olive oil. Griddle the polenta slices for 2 to 3 minutes on each side, until they begin to color slightly. If cooking in batches, keep warm in a low oven.

To serve, place the griddled polenta slices on warm plates and top with the sautéed mushrooms. Scatter over shavings of pecorino and the remaining oregano leaves and serve immediately.

Shaping
ravioli

Lay one sheet of pasta on a clean counter, with a long edge toward you. Place teaspoonfuls of the filling along one half of the sheet (closest to you), leaving about $^3/_4$ inch (2cm) between the filling mounds and a $1^1/_4$-inch (3cm) margin at the edge. Lightly brush the area around the filling and the rest of the pasta sheet with egg wash. Fold the edge of the pasta over the filling to enclose the mounds and press the pasta down around them to seal and exclude any air gaps. Fold the pasta over again and press down between the mounds of filling. Using a fluted pasta cutter or sharp knife, cut between the filling molds to make the ravioli. Repeat with the rest and keep covered with a clean dish towel until ready to cook.

Spinach, ricotta, and pine nut ravioli with sage butter

MAKING RAVIOLI IS TRULY SATISFYING and fun—especially if you get others involved. In Italy, this typically happens, with the matriarch in charge of quality control. You should have enough filling here for about 20 ravioli. Any pasta dough that isn't used can be rerolled into thin sheets and cut into thick strips to make pappardelle or tagliatelle.

SERVES 4–5

Pasta dough:
pinch of saffron strands
1 tbsp (15ml) boiling water
4 cups (550g) Italian "00" flour
1/4 tsp (1ml) fine sea salt
4 medium eggs, plus 6 egg yolks
2 tbsp (30ml) olive oil

Filling:
2 tbsp (30ml) olive oil
2 garlic cloves, peeled and minced
1lb (500g) spinach leaves
1 tbsp (15ml) butter
1/4 tsp (1ml) freshly grated
   nutmeg
sea salt and black pepper
2/3 cup (150g) ricotta cheese
2 3/4oz (75g) Parmesan, grated
2/3 cup (75g) pine nuts, toasted
squeeze of lemon juice, to taste
beaten egg, for brushing

Sage butter:
5 tbsp (75ml) butter, diced
2 tbsp (30ml) heavy cream
6 sage sprigs, leaves shredded

To serve:
Parmesan, for grating

For the pasta, lightly crush the saffron in a bowl, pour on the boiling water, and let infuse until cooled. Put the rest of the ingredients into a food processor, add the saffron water, and whiz until the mix resembles coarse crumbs; add a little more water if needed. Tip into a bowl and press into a ball. Turn onto a lightly floured counter and knead until smooth. The dough should be soft but not sticky; if it feels too wet, knead in a little more flour. Wrap in plastic wrap and chill for 30 minutes.

To make the filling, heat the olive oil in a large skillet and pan-fry the garlic until lightly golden. Add the spinach and cook for 2 to 3 minutes until the liquid released has been absorbed. Increase the heat slightly and stir in the butter, nutmeg, and seasoning. Drain and roughly chop the spinach. In a large bowl, beat together the ricotta, Parmesan, and toasted pine nuts. Stir in the spinach and a touch of lemon juice. Taste and adjust the seasoning if necessary, then cover and chill for at least 30 minutes.

Cut the pasta into 8 pieces, roll into balls, and keep each wrapped until needed. Using a pasta machine, roll each ball into a long sheet, about 32 by 5 inches (80 by 13cm), passing it through the rollers and narrowing the setting gradually until you reach the thinnest setting. Cover with a damp dish towel. To shape the ravioli, follow my guide (on the preceding pages).

For the sage butter, melt the butter in a saucepan and heat until it begins to brown. Take off the heat and let stand for 1 minute, then strain through a strainer into a clean pan. Heat slowly, then stir in the cream and sage.

Bring a large pan of lightly salted water to a boil, add the ravioli, and cook for 2 to 3 minutes. Drain well and toss with the sage butter. Grate over a little extra Parmesan and serve at once.

5 ways with pizza

Pizza bases

Using an electric mixer fitted with a dough hook, mix 3$\frac{1}{2}$ cups (500g) strong all-purpose flour with a $\frac{1}{4}$-oz (7g) sachet fast-action dried yeast, 1 tsp (5ml) fine sea salt, and generous $\frac{1}{3}$ cup (100ml) warm water. Slowly add more water (up to $\frac{2}{3}$ cup/150ml) just until the dough starts to come together. Knead in the mixer for 1 minute, then briefly on a lightly floured counter until smooth and elastic. Transfer to an oiled bowl, cover with plastic wrap, and let rise in a warm place until doubled in size. Knead briefly on a floured counter, then divide in half and roll each piece out to an 8-inch (20cm) circle. Place on an oiled baking tray.

MAKES 2

Tomato sauce

Gently sauté 2 minced garlic cloves and 1 minced onion in 2 tbsp (30ml) olive oil in a medium pan until softened. Add a 14oz (400g) can chopped tomatoes, $\frac{1}{2}$ cup (100g) diced cherry tomatoes, and 1 tbsp (15ml) tomato paste. Simmer gently for 40 minutes or until reduced and quite thick.

Pizza **Margherita**

Heat the oven to 425°F (220°C). Spread the tomato sauce (see left) over the pizza bases, top with 8oz (250g) thinly sliced mozzarella, and scatter over some basil leaves. Season well and drizzle lightly with olive oil. Bake for 15 to 20 minutes until the crust is golden. MAKES 2

Prosciutto and marinated **artichoke pizza**

Heat the oven to 425°F (220°C). Melt 4 tsp (20g) butter in a pan and add 14oz (400g) quartered plum tomatoes, 1 finely diced red chile, a handful of chopped oregano leaves, 1 tsp (5ml) sugar, and some seasoning. Cook for 5 to 7 minutes, then stir in 1 tsp (5ml) red wine vinegar. Cool slightly. Spoon the cooked tomato mixture over the pizza bases and top each with 6–8 finely sliced marinated artichokes, a few slices of prosciutto, and a handful of black olives. Drizzle over a little olive oil and season lightly. Bake for 15 to 20 minutes until the crust is golden. Serve topped with a handful of shaved Parmesan and a scattering of arugula. MAKES 2

Pizza bianca with **four cheeses**

Heat the oven to 350°F (180°C). Put 8 large unpeeled garlic cloves in an ovenproof dish. Drizzle with olive oil, season, and roast for 20 to 25 minutes until soft. Squeeze the soft flesh from the skins into a bowl and mash with 1 tbsp (15ml) minced rosemary, 3–4 tbsp (45–60ml) truffle oil (or olive oil), and some seasoning. Increase the oven temperature to 425°F (220°C). Spread the garlic paste thinly over the pizza bases and top each with a generous handful of freshly grated Parmesan, goat cheese, and Gorgonzola, and a few mozzarella slices. Bake for 15 to 20 minutes until the crust is golden. MAKES 2

Roasted **tomato** and **mushroom pizza**

Heat the oven to 350°F (180°C). Place $2/3$lb–14oz (350–400g) cherry tomatoes on a baking tray, drizzle with 2 tbsp (30ml) olive oil, and season with salt and pepper. Roast for 8 to 10 minutes until the tomatoes are soft but still holding their shape; remove and set aside. Increase the oven temperature to 425°F (220°C). Melt 4 tsp (20g) butter in a skillet and sauté 3 cups (225g) sliced mixed mushrooms with 1 tsp (5ml) chopped thyme leaves over medium-high heat for 4 to 6 minutes until softened and any moisture released has cooked off. Cool slightly. Spread the tomato sauce (see left) over the pizza bases. Top with the sautéed mushrooms, 4oz (120g) goat cheese, 4oz (120g) thinly sliced mozzarella, and the roasted cherry tomatoes. Drizzle with olive oil and season well. Bake for 15 to 20 minutes until the crust is golden. MAKES 2

Mini **salami** and **roasted pepper pizzas**

Heat the oven to 425°F (220°C). Blitz $1/2$ x 12oz (350g) jar roasted peppers with 2 chopped garlic cloves, $1/2$ cup (50g) freshly grated Parmesan, $1/4$ cup (35g) toasted pine nuts, a handful of basil leaves, generous $1/3$ cup (100ml) extra-virgin olive oil, and some seasoning to a paste in a food processor. Using a $2^1/_2$-inch (6cm) cookie cutter, cut the pizza dough into circles. Spread each with a little red pepper paste, then top with the remaining roasted peppers (from the jar) and a slice of spicy salami. Sprinkle with Parmesan and bake for 12 to 15 minutes until the crust is golden. MAKES 14

Seafood risotto

GOOD RISOTTO RICE AND A FLAVORFUL STOCK are essential for a superb risotto. For this one, I've enhanced the flavor of the fish stock with the juices from a pan of steamed mussels. The mussels are shelled and added to the rice at the end. I've kept the seafood to a simple trio of mussels, shrimp, and squid, but feel free to serve the risotto topped with a pan-fried fillet of porgy, red snapper, or bream.

SERVES 6–8

10oz (300g) live mussels, scrubbed clean and debearded
generous $3/4$ cup (200ml) water
$1 1/4$ cups (300ml) dry white wine
$3 1/3$ cups (800ml) fish or chicken stock
pinch of saffron strands
2 tbsp (30ml) olive oil
3 tbsp (40ml) butter
1 small head of fennel, trimmed and minced
1 shallot, peeled and minced
1 garlic clove, peeled and minced
2 cups (350g) risotto rice, such as Arborio, Carnaroli, or Vialone Nano
10oz (300g) peeled raw shrimp
7oz (200g) baby squid, cleaned and sliced
finely grated zest of 1 lemon
sea salt and black pepper
handful of Italian parsley, leaves chopped

Check over the mussels, discarding any that are cracked or open and do not close when sharply tapped. Pour the water and generous $3/4$ cup (200ml) of the wine into a large saucepan and bring to a boil over high heat. Tip in the mussels, cover the pan with a tight-fitting lid, and give it a few shakes. Cook for 2 to 3 minutes until the mussels have opened. Drain them in a colander set on top of a saucepan to collect the juices. Shell the mussels and set aside, discarding any that remain closed. Add the stock and saffron strands to the mussel juices and bring to a simmer; keep it at low simmer.

Meanwhile, heat the olive oil and half the butter in a large saucepan. Add the fennel, shallot, and garlic and cook until softened but not colored, about 6 to 8 minutes. Tip the rice into the pan, stir well to coat, and cook for about 2 minutes until the rice starts to turn translucent. Pour in the remaining wine and let bubble until all the liquid has been absorbed. Add a ladleful of hot stock and stir until it is all absorbed. Continue adding the stock in this way, a ladleful at a time, until the rice is creamy with a slight bite. (You may not need all the stock.)

Stir the shrimp and squid into the risotto and simmer for 2 minutes until they are just cooked through, adding the mussels for the last minute. Finally, stir in the grated lemon zest and remaining butter and taste for seasoning. Take the pan off the heat and let stand for a few minutes.

Divide the risotto between warm serving bowls and sprinkle with the chopped parsley. Serve at once.

Stuffed red mullet
with roasted new potatoes

THIS IS A GREAT WAY TO SAVOR RED MULLET, a popular fish around the Mediterranean. Get your fish supplier to scale, clean, and butterfly the red mullet, leaving the tails intact. This way, you can neatly stuff each fish with the tasty black olive and anchovy paste. Depending on the size of the fish, you may have some paste left over —keep it in a jar in the refrigerator and use to flavor other fish or chicken dishes.

SERVES 4

4 red mullet, about 1lb (500g) each, butterflied
1^2/$_3$ cups (200g) black olives, pitted
4 anchovy fillets in oil, drained
12 sun-dried tomatoes
2 garlic cloves, peeled and roughly chopped
5 tbsp (75ml) olive oil, plus extra to oil
sea salt and black pepper

Roasted potatoes:
2lb (1kg) small new potatoes, halved
2 lemons, cut into small wedges
few rosemary sprigs, leaves stripped
6 garlic cloves, with skin on
3 tbsp (45ml) olive oil

First, roast the new potatoes. Preheat the oven to 400°F (200°C). Tip the potatoes, lemons, rosemary, garlic, and olive oil into a large baking dish. Season with salt and pepper and toss well. Roast in the oven for about an hour until the potatoes are crisp on the outside and soft and fluffy in the middle.

About 20 minutes before the potatoes will be ready, rinse the fish cavities and carefully pat dry. Put the olives, anchovies, sun-dried tomatoes, garlic, and 2 tbsp (30ml) of the olive oil into a blender and blitz to a wet paste.

Generously stuff the fish cavities with the olive and anchovy paste, then rub the remaining olive oil all over the skins and season with salt and pepper. Lay the fish on a lightly oiled baking tray and roast in the oven for 15 to 20 minutes, depending on their thickness, until just cooked through—they should feel just firm when lightly pressed.

Divide the roasted potatoes between warm plates and place a stuffed red mullet alongside. Serve a lightly dressed green salad on the side.

Pappardelle with **rabbit** ragù

EMILIA-ROMAGNA IS HOME to some of the finest Italian cooking, not least this wonderfully tasty rabbit dish. I'm using farmed rabbit here, for its tender meat, but you can use a wild one for a stronger, gamier flavor if you prefer, allowing an extra 15 to 20 minutes braising time. You should be able to buy fresh pappardelle from a good Italian deli—or, of course, you can make your own. Otherwise, use good dried pasta.

SERVES 4

3 tbsp (45ml) olive oil
1 farmed rabbit, jointed into
    8 pieces
sea salt and black pepper
3 garlic cloves, peeled and
    chopped
2 onions, peeled and chopped
1 fennel bulb, trimmed and
    chopped
1 carrot, peeled and chopped
3oz (85g) pancetta, diced
1 tbsp (15ml) juniper berries,
    lightly crushed
2 rosemary sprigs, leaves picked
    and minced
2 thyme sprigs, leaves picked
generous 1 cup (250ml) red wine
2 tbsp (30ml) tomato paste
1¼ cups (300ml) chicken stock
1 tbsp (15ml) grainy mustard
1lb (500g) fresh pappardelle or
    tagliatelle
handful of Italian parsley, leaves
    roughly chopped
freshly grated Parmesan, to serve

Heat the olive oil in a large, wide heavy pan. Season the rabbit pieces with salt and pepper and pan-fry them for 2 minutes on each side until browned. Remove with a slotted spoon to a plate.

Add the garlic, onions, fennel, and carrot to the pan. Pan-fry over high heat for 2 to 3 minutes until slightly softened, then add the pancetta and continue to cook until it is lightly browned, about 6 to 8 minutes.

Add the juniper berries, rosemary, and thyme, then return the browned rabbit pieces to the pan. Add the wine and tomato paste and let bubble until the liquid has reduced by half. Stir in the stock, season, and put the lid on. Cook for 20 to 30 minutes until the rabbit is tender.

Take out the rabbit pieces and place on a board. When cool enough to handle, remove the meat from the bones, shredding larger pieces as necessary. If the sauce is very thin, simmer it until thickened to a light coating consistency. Return the rabbit meat to the sauce and heat through. Stir in the mustard, taste, and adjust the seasoning.

When almost ready to serve, bring a large saucepan of salted water to a boil. Add the pasta and cook for a few minutes until al dente. Drain well and toss with the rabbit ragù, making sure the pasta is nicely coated with the sauce.

Divide between warm serving plates and spoon over any remaining ragù. Scatter over some parsley leaves and serve with grated Parmesan for sprinkling over.

Osso buco with roasted butternut squash and creamy polenta

LITERALLY MEANING "HOLE IN THE BONE," this classic dish of braised veal shanks hails from Milan. Many insist that the original version did not include tomatoes, but over the years they have been introduced, creating a distinctive brownish red sauce. When ordering the veal, inform your butcher that you are making osso buco so he can supply you with the proper cut of veal shank.

SERVES 4

4 pieces veal shank (bone-in),
   1¹/₂–2 inches (4–5cm) thick
3 tbsp (25ml) all-purpose flour
sea salt and black pepper
3 tbsp (45ml) olive oil
2 onions, peeled and chopped
3 garlic cloves, peeled and sliced
³/₄ cup (200ml) dry white wine
3 thyme sprigs
3 rosemary sprigs
1 bay leaf
1 cup (225ml) strained tomatoes
1 cup (250ml) chicken stock
handful of Italian parsley leaves

Roasted butternut squash:
1 large butternut squash
2–3 tbsp (30–45ml) olive oil
2 garlic cloves, peeled and sliced
2 thyme or rosemary sprigs,
   leaves stripped

Creamy polenta:
scant 1 cup (100g) instant polenta
3¹/₂ cups (750ml) water
1¹/₂ tbsp (20g) butter
1oz (30g) Parmesan, grated
1 tbsp (15ml) mascarpone
squeeze of lemon juice, to taste

Preheat the oven to 400°F (200°C). Lay the veal pieces on a board. Season the flour with salt and pepper and use to lightly coat the veal. Heat the olive oil in a large, wide heavy pan or ovenproof casserole and brown the veal pieces in batches, turning them to color all over; set aside on a plate.

Add the onions to the pan and cook for 2 to 3 minutes, then add the garlic. Cook until the onions are soft and golden, then pour in the wine and add the thyme, rosemary, and bay leaf. Let bubble until the liquid has reduced by two-thirds. Stir in the tomatoes, season with salt and pepper, and cook for 2 to 3 minutes. Pour in the stock, cover with a lid, and cook in the oven for 1¹/₂ hours, turning the meat halfway through cooking.

Meanwhile, peel and seed the squash, then cut into small chunks. Place in a large bowl with the olive oil, garlic, thyme or rosemary, and some salt and pepper. Toss well, then transfer to a baking tray. When the osso buco has been cooking for about 50 minutes, place the tray of squash in the oven and roast for about 40 minutes until tender.

In the meantime, prepare the polenta. Pour the water into a large pan, add a pinch of salt, and bring to a boil. Slowly whisk in the polenta and keep stirring for about 5 minutes until it thickens and has absorbed all of the water. Remove from the heat and stir in the butter, Parmesan, mascarpone, and lemon juice to taste. Season with pepper and a little more salt to taste, if needed. Keep warm until ready to serve.

Discard the thyme, rosemary, and bay leaf from the osso buco. Pile the creamy polenta onto warm plates and top with the osso buco. Finish with a sprinkling of parsley and serve the roasted squash alongside.

Caramelized peaches with vin santo

PEACHES ARE OFTEN PAIRED WITH WINE in Italy—as an aperitif, I am partial to a peach bellini. I also enjoy them baked with a traditional almondy stuffing and served topped with a prosecco-flavored zabaglione. Here is an effortless way to transform ripe peaches into a lovely dessert. If you don't have any vin santo, use a sweet Marsala wine or a splash of amaretto liqueur, whatever you have to hand.

SERVES 4

½ cup (100g) granulated or superfine sugar
3 tbsp (45ml) water
1 vanilla bean, slit open
generous ⅓ cup (100ml) vin santo
3½ tbsp (50g) unsalted butter, softened
8 firm but ripe peaches, pitted and quartered
good-quality vanilla ice cream, to serve

Put the sugar and water into a medium heavy saucepan (that will hold the peaches) over medium-low heat. Once the sugar has dissolved, increase the heat and cook the syrup to a light caramel color. Remove from the heat. Scrape the seeds from the vanilla bean directly into the pan and stir in the vin santo and butter.

Return the pan to medium heat and stir the sauce until it is smooth. Add the peaches and cook for a few minutes until they have softened slightly but are still holding their shape. Take the pan off the heat.

Divide the peaches and sauce between serving bowls and top each one with a generous scoop of very cold vanilla ice cream. Serve at once.

Marsala roasted figs
with zabaglione

RIPE, JUICY FIGS IN SEASON are transformed to an elegant dessert with this simple recipe. The figs acquire additional sweetness and a sophisticated depth of flavor from the Marsala.

SERVES 4

softened butter, for greasing
8 ripe figs
3 tbsp (45ml) Marsala wine
1/4 cup (50g) soft brown sugar
grated zest and juice of 1/2 orange
handful of pistachios, toasted
   and chopped

Zabaglione:
4 large egg yolks
1/2 cup (60g) confectioners' sugar,
   sifted
finely grated zest of 1 lemon
5 tbsp (75ml) Marsala wine

Preheat the oven to 300°F (150°C). Generously butter a shallow ovenproof dish large enough to hold the figs. Trim the stalks, then slash the top of each fig in a crisscross fashion and gently squeeze the base to open the fruit slightly. Stand the figs in the buttered dish.

In a small bowl, mix together the Marsala, brown sugar, orange zest, and juice. Spoon this mixture over the figs and roast in the oven for 10 minutes. Take out the dish and baste the figs with the pan juices, then return to the oven for another 5 minutes.

To make the zabaglione, put the egg yolks and confectioners' sugar into a large heatproof bowl and set over a pan of barely simmering water. Using a handheld electric whisk, slowly and steadily whisk the mixture until it turns pale, thick, and creamy; take care to avoid overheating. At this point, increase the whisking speed. Add the lemon zest and then gradually whisk in the Marsala. Continue to whisk for another 10 minutes or so, until the zabaglione is thick and foamy, and the mixture leaves a trail when the beaters are lifted above the surface. Take the bowl off the pan and let the zabaglione cool slightly, whisking occasionally.

To serve, spoon the zabaglione over the roasted figs and sprinkle with the chopped pistachios. Serve while still warm.

Amaretto and
chocolate torte

THIS IRRESISTIBLE CHOCOLATE TORTE
has a rich, melt-in-the-mouth texture. It makes
a fantastic dessert for entertaining because you
can cook it ahead of time and keep it chilled—just
remember to take it out of the refrigerator about
30 minutes before serving to enjoy it at its best.

SERVES 8

softened butter, for greasing
2/3lb (350g) dark chocolate
　　(about 60% cocoa solids)
6 tbsp (90ml) Amaretto di Saronno
　　liqueur
4 large eggs, separated
1 3/4oz (50g) amaretti cookies,
　　finely crushed
1 cup (200g) superfine sugar
cocoa powder, to dust
lightly whipped cream or
　　mascarpone, to serve

Preheat the oven to 350°F (180°C). Butter an 8-inch (20cm) round cake pan with removable base and line the base with waxed paper.

Break the chocolate into pieces, place in a heatproof bowl, and set over a pan of barely simmering water. As it begins to melt, stir in the liqueur. When the chocolate has completely melted and is smooth, remove from the heat and set aside to cool slightly.

Beat the egg yolks together in large bowl until thick and creamy. Mix the crushed amaretti into the chocolate mixture, then stir in the egg yolks.

In a separate clean bowl, whisk the egg whites to soft peaks using a handheld electric whisk. Now whisk in the superfine sugar, a tablespoonful at a time, until you have a firm glossy meringue. Fold the egg whites into the chocolate mixture, a third at a time.

Spoon the mixture into the prepared pan and gently smooth the surface. Bake in the oven for 35 to 40 minutes until the torte is risen and the top is slightly crusty. The surface may crack, but the middle should be lovely and moist. Turn off the oven and let the torte cool slowly inside for at least an hour.

Remove the torte from the oven and allow to cool completely before unmolding. Transfer to a large serving plate and dust with cocoa powder. Serve, cut into slices, with lightly whipped cream or mascarpone.

GREEK

GREEK FOOD IS OFTEN UNDERESTIMATED AND CAN
BE QUITE DELICIOUS. ESSENTIALLY A SIMPLE STYLE
OF COOKING, IT DRAWS CLOSELY FROM WHAT IS GROWN
LOCALLY AND FISHED FROM THE SEA. HERBS SUCH AS
ROSEMARY AND OREGANO GROW EVERYWHERE IN THE
HILLS AND ARE USED ABUNDANTLY, AND THE BEES
THAT FEED OFF THE POLLEN MAKE DELECTABLE
HONEY, WHICH ALSO FEATURES STRONGLY IN COOKING.
FETA IS THE MOST COMMONLY USED CHEESE AND
I LOVE THE CRUMBLY TEXTURE AND LOVELY SALTINESS
IT LENDS A DISH. MOST OF US PROBABLY THINK OF
MOUSSAKA AS THE MOST TYPICAL GREEK DISH AND
I'VE INCLUDED A RECIPE FOR IT HERE, BUT THERE'S
MORE TO GREEK FOOD ... IT'S NOT ALL ABOUT KEBABS.

Taramasalata with homemade pita

A STAPLE GREEK MEZE DISH, taramasalata is easy to buy, but commercially produced taramasalata—invariably tainted pink with food coloring—tastes nothing like the real thing. Pure, homemade taramasalata has an intense flavor of smoked cod's roe, which can be mellowed by adjusting the amount of olive oil. At the restaurants, we make our dip with a hefty amount of good olive oil to get a very smooth, creamy texture—much like a thick mayonnaise.

SERVES 6

2½ thick slices of white bread, crusts removed
generous ⅓ cup (100ml) whole milk
7oz (200g) smoked cod's roe
1 garlic clove, peeled and crushed
juice of 1½ lemons
sea salt and black pepper
scant 1¼ cups (275ml) light olive oil
a little milk (if needed)
extra-virgin olive oil, to drizzle

Pita bread:
3¼ cups (450g) strong white flour, plus extra to dust
1 tsp (5ml) fine sea salt
2 x ¼-oz (7g) sachets active dry yeast
1 tbsp (15ml) extra-virgin olive oil, plus extra to oil the bowl
1¼ cups (300ml) tepid water

First, make the pita dough. Mix the flour, salt, and yeast together in a large bowl. Make a well in the center and pour in the extra-virgin olive oil and most of the water. Stir to bring the mixture together into a ball, adding a little more water as necessary to get a soft, but not sticky, dough. Tip out onto a lightly floured counter and knead for 10 minutes until smooth. Put the dough in a lightly oiled clean bowl, cover with plastic wrap, and let rise in a warm place for about 2 hours.

To make the taramasalata, tear the bread into small pieces, place in a bowl, pour over the milk, and set aside to soak. Cut away any hard bits of skin from the cod's roe, then place the roe in a food processor along with the garlic, lemon juice, and a good grinding of pepper. Add the soaked bread and blend to a smooth paste. With the motor running, gradually trickle in the light olive oil through the funnel. Taste and adjust the seasoning with salt and pepper and add a touch more milk if the taramasalata seems too oily. Spoon into a bowl.

When the pita dough has roughly doubled in size, punch it down and knead briefly on a lightly floured counter for a minute. Divide into 12 equal pieces and shape into balls. Let prove in a warm place for 15 minutes. Meanwhile, preheat the oven to 400°F (200°C) and put 2 lightly oiled baking trays inside to heat. Roll each dough ball out into an oval, ⅛ inch (2–3mm) thick. Transfer to the warmed baking trays and bake in the oven for 6 to 8 minutes until puffed up and light golden in color.

Drizzle a little extra-virgin olive oil over the surface of the taramasalata before serving, with the warm pita breads.

Griddled haloumi
and **eggplant** salad

HALOUMI IS A CYPRIOT CHEESE traditionally made from a combination of goat's and ewe's milk. However, many commercial varieties now include cow's milk, which produces an inferior cheese. Do try to get hold of an authentic haloumi—the flavor and texture will make all the difference to this lovely salad. If you have any olive dressing left over, keep it in a jar in the refrigerator to use for drizzling over broiled fish or lamb.

SERVES 6

1 large eggplant
sea salt and black pepper
6 ripe plum tomatoes
1/3 cup (40g) kalamata olives, pitted
small bunch of mint, leaves shredded
olive oil, for brushing
1lb (500g) haloumi
2–3 tbsp (30–45ml) all-purpose flour

Olive dressing:
scant 2/3 cup (75g) kalamata olives, pitted
3 tbsp (45ml) red wine vinegar
1 tsp (5ml) dried oregano
5 tbsp (75ml) olive oil
5 tbsp (75ml) peanut oil

Cut the eggplant into thin slices. Place in a colander, sprinkle lightly with salt, and let stand for 20 minutes. (The salt will help to draw out excess moisture from the eggplant.) Pat dry with paper towels.

Cut the tomatoes into wedges and put into a large bowl with the olives and mint. Set aside while you make the dressing.

For the dressing, tip the olives, wine vinegar, and dried oregano into a blender and blitz to a smooth purée. With the motor running, gradually pour in the olive and peanut oils and season well with salt and pepper to taste. Transfer to a jar and set aside.

About 15 minutes before you will be ready to serve, put a griddle pan over high heat. Brush the eggplant slices with olive oil and griddle for about 2 minutes on each side until softened and slightly charred. Add to the bowl of tomatoes, pour over some of the dressing, and toss to coat.

Thinly slice the haloumi and lightly coat with flour. Griddle the slices until they are turning golden brown around the edges and just starting to melt.

To serve, arrange the griddled eggplant on a large platter and top with the haloumi. Spoon the tomato and olive salad on top and drizzle over a little more olive dressing. Serve at once, while the haloumi is still warm.

White bean and vegetable soup

KNOWN AS *FASOULADA* **IN GREECE,** this is a wonderfully sustaining and economical soup. It's very easy to prepare—you just need to remember to put the beans to soak the night before, and allow for a couple of hours simmering on the stove. Serve with country bread as a wholesome lunch, or in small bowls as a rustic appetizer.

SERVES 4–6

scant 3 cups (500g) dried white beans, such as
    haricot beans or Greek *fasolia gigantes*, soaked
    overnight in plenty of cold water
3–4 tbsp (45–60ml) olive oil
2 carrots, peeled and minced
1 large onion, peeled and minced
2 celery stalks, peeled and minced
2 garlic cloves, peeled and minced
sea salt and black pepper
6 ripe plum tomatoes, skinned, seeded, and
    minced
1 tbsp (15ml) tomato paste
1 tsp (5ml) dried oregano
small handful of Italian parsley, leaves chopped

To serve (optional):
extra-virgin olive oil, to drizzle
crumbled feta, to finish

Drain the white beans, tip into a large saucepan, and pour over fresh cold water to cover generously. Bring to a boil over medium heat and skim off the scum and froth from the surface. Lower the heat and simmer for about an hour.

Heat the olive oil in another saucepan. Add the carrots, onion, celery, garlic, and some seasoning. Cook, stirring frequently, over medium-high heat for 6 to 8 minutes until the vegetables begin to soften. Add the chopped tomatoes, tomato paste, and dried oregano. Stir over the heat for another minute or two, then tip the contents of the pan into the pot of beans.

Add a little more water if necessary to ensure that everything is covered and simmer for another 30 to 45 minutes until the beans are soft. If the soup becomes too thick, dilute it with a splash of hot water.

To serve, ladle the soup into warm bowls and scatter over the chopped parsley. If you wish, drizzle each bowl with a little extra-virgin olive oil and top with the some crumbled feta. Serve hot.

Barbecuing sardines

Sardines take on a lovely smoky flavor on the barbecue, so I'll invariably opt to cook them this way if I possibly can. The secret to a successful barbecue is to make sure that the fire is not too hot when you put the food on the grill. The coals should be gray and ashen with a good heat rising above.

Barbecued sardines with tzatziki

TZATZIKI MAY BE A SURPRISING accompaniment to sardines, but I find it works well as the acidity from the lemon juice and yogurt helps to counter the oiliness of the fish. Make it an hour or two in advance to allow time for the flavors to develop.

SERVES 4–6

12 very fresh sardines,
   scaled and cleaned
olive oil, to drizzle
sea salt and black pepper

Tzatziki:
1 cucumber
2 garlic cloves, peeled and grated
1 1/2 cups (350g) Greek yogurt
juice of 1/2 lemon, or to taste
2 tbsp (30ml) extra-virgin olive oil

To serve:
extra-virgin olive oil, to drizzle
small handful of mint leaves,
   chopped

To prepare the tzatziki, peel the cucumber, cut in half lengthwise, and scrape out the seeds. Coarsely grate the flesh, sprinkle with 1 tsp (5ml) salt, and place in a strainer set over a bowl. Let drain for an hour or so, then squeeze out as much excess water from the flesh as possible, using your hands.

Mix the grated cucumber, garlic, yogurt, lemon juice, and extra-virgin olive oil together in a bowl. Season with salt and pepper to taste, then cover and refrigerate.

Light the barbecue and wait for the fire to burn down to gray embers (see preceding pages). Or, if you are cooking indoors, heat a griddle pan until hot. Rinse the sardines and pat dry, then rub all over with a little olive oil and some salt and pepper. Place the sardines on the grill (or griddle) and cook for about 3 minutes on each side until the flesh feels firm, but still comes away from the bone easily.

Pile the hot sardines onto a platter and serve with the tzatziki on the side. Finish with a drizzle of extra-virgin olive oil and a scattering of chopped mint.

Squid stuffed with tomato and herb rice

THIS IS A VERY TASTY ONE-POT DISH. Baby squid are stuffed with a mixture of rice, tomatoes, onions, and fresh herbs and any extra stuffing is added to the pan to cook alongside. For a little touch of sweetness and extra texture, add a handful of raisins and pine nuts to the rice mixture. You can also throw a couple of chopped tomatoes into the sauce to give it a little acidity.

SERVES 5

10 baby squid, cleaned, tentacles
    reserved
olive oil, to drizzle

Rice stuffing:
2 tbsp (30ml) olive oil
1 red onion, peeled and minced
2 garlic cloves, peeled and minced
generous $1/3$ cup (100ml) dry
    white wine
$1^1/2$ cups (300g) long-grain white
    rice
4 plum tomatoes, skinned,
    seeded, and diced
1 tsp (5ml) superfine sugar
sea salt and black pepper
$3^1/2$ cups (850ml) water
handful of mint, leaves chopped
handful of Italian parsley, leaves
    chopped, plus extra to finish

First, prepare the stuffing. Heat the olive oil in a wide pan over medium heat and add the onion and garlic. Sauté gently for 6 to 8 minutes until softened but not colored. Increase the heat slightly and pour in the wine. Let bubble until the liquid has reduced by half, then add the rice to the pan and cook for a minute, stirring continuously.

Next, add the tomatoes, sugar, and some salt and pepper. Pour in $2^1/2$ cups (600ml) water, then cover with a lid and let simmer for 12 to 15 minutes, or until the water has been absorbed and the rice is fluffy. Remove from the heat and let stand for 5 minutes. Fluff up the rice with a fork, then allow to cool, before stirring in the chopped mint and parsley.

Preheat the oven to 350°F (180°C). Carefully stuff the squid pouches with the rice mixture and thread a toothpick through the top of each one to hold in the stuffing. Lay the stuffed squid in an oiled ovenproof dish.

Add the tentacles and any remaining rice stuffing to the dish and pour the remaining generous 1 cup (250ml) water over the top. Drizzle with a little olive oil. Bake in the oven for 30 to 35 minutes until the squid is tender and cooked through. Scatter over some chopped parsley to serve.

Walnut cake

DRENCHED IN A FRAGRANT SPICE SYRUP as soon as it comes out of the oven, this classic cake is delectably moist. It is known as *karydopita* in Greece and is often made without any flour, although I find adding a little makes for a lighter cake. It is best served with a generous dollop of Greek yogurt and some strong Greek tea or coffee to counteract the sweetness.

SERVES 4

softened butter, for greasing
5 large eggs, separated
2 tbsp (30ml) brandy
grated zest and juice of 1 orange
scant $^1/_2$ cup (90g) superfine sugar
$^1/_2$ tsp (2ml) ground cinnamon
$^1/_4$ tsp (1ml) ground cloves
$2^1/_2$ tbsp (20ml) self-rising flour, sifted
2 tsp (10ml) baking powder
scant $^1/_2$ cup (35g) day-old white bread crumbs
$1^1/_2$ cups (175g) walnut pieces

Spice syrup:
scant $^2/_3$ cup (125g) superfine sugar
$^2/_3$ cup (150ml) water
3 cloves
1 cinnamon stick
juice and thinly pared zest of 1 lemon

Preheat the oven to 375°F (190°C). Butter and line the base and sides of a 9-inch (23cm) cake pan, preferably with a removable base.

In a large bowl, beat together the egg yolks, brandy, orange zest, and juice until smooth and creamy.

Put the sugar, cinnamon, cloves, flour, baking powder, bread crumbs, and $1^1/_4$ cups (150g) of the walnuts into a food processor and blitz to fine crumbs. Tip the mixture into a large mixing bowl. In a separate, clean bowl, whisk the egg whites to firm peaks.

Fold the egg yolk mixture into the crumb mixture, then carefully fold in the egg whites, using a large metal spoon, until evenly incorporated.

Pour the cake batter into the prepared pan and bake in the oven for 40 minutes. To test, insert a skewer into the center—if it comes out clean then the cake is done, if not return to the oven for a few more minutes.

Make the spice syrup while the cake is in the oven. Put all the ingredients into a small saucepan and stir over medium heat until the sugar is dissolved. Bring to a boil and then simmer for 5 minutes. Let cool completely before straining through a strainer into a pitcher. Chop or crush the remaining walnuts into small pieces.

Once the cake is ready, remove from the oven and prick all over with a thin skewer. Sprinkle over the remaining walnuts, then spoon the cold syrup over the hot cake. Allow to cool before unmolding and serving.

Pan-fried **watermelon** with **yogurt** and caramelized **walnuts**

SWEET, JUICY WATERMELONS ARE MUCH LOVED by the Greeks. When this refreshing fruit is at its peak toward the end of August, it often appears at breakfast, with feta and olives in lunchtime salads, and, of course, as a dessert. I like to pan-fry watermelon slices to bring out their natural sweetness—and serve them topped with honey caramelized walnuts and thick yogurt for a tempting dessert.

SERVES 4

1 small or $^1/_2$ medium watermelon
a little olive oil
confectioners' sugar, to dust
1$^3/_4$–2 cups (400–500g) Greek
    yogurt

Caramelized walnuts:
1 tbsp (15ml) butter
scant $^1/_4$ cup (65g) runny honey
scant 1 cup (100g) walnuts

To prepare the caramelized walnuts, line a baking tray with waxed paper. Put the butter and honey into a small heavy saucepan and place over medium heat for 2 to 3 minutes until the butter has melted. Now add the walnuts, stirring to coat well. Continue to heat for another minute or two until the mixture starts to bubble and turn golden brown. Carefully tip onto the lined baking tray and set aside for 1 to 2 hours until set. (Don't expect the caramelized nuts to be brittle like praline, as they have a softer set.) Break into small pieces with your hands and store in an airtight container until needed.

When almost ready to serve, cut the watermelon into 1$^1/_4$–1$^1/_2$-inch (3–4cm) thick triangles or squares. Heat a little olive oil in a nonstick skillet over high heat. You will need to pan-fry the watermelon in batches. Dust the slices on both sides with confectioners' sugar, then pan-fry for 1 to 1$^1/_2$ minutes on each side. Remove to a warm plate and repeat with the rest.

Place a pan-fried watermelon slice on each plate, add a generous dollop of yogurt, and scatter over the caramelized walnuts. Serve at once.

SPANISH

I LOVE GOING TO SPAIN AND I'VE SPENT A LOT OF TIME IN SAN SEBASTIÁN. ARZAK, THE RENOWNED FAMILY-RUN RESTAURANT IN THE CITY, HEADED BY JUAN MARI ARZAK, HOLDS 3 MICHELIN STARS. CATALONIA, OF COURSE, IS THE HOME OF FERRAN ADRIÀ'S FAMOUS EL BULLI RESTAURANT, WHERE THE FOOD NEVER CEASES TO AMAZE ME. BUT WHAT REALLY DRAWS ME TO SPANISH FOOD IS THE SIMPLE RUSTIC PLEASURES—A GREAT PAELLA OR SOME SIMPLY COOKED FISH OR SHELLFISH, PERHAPS. AND I ADORE THE SPANISH TAPAS CUSTOM. IT WAS THE INSPIRATION FOR OUR MAZE RESTAURANT, WHERE SMALL PLATES ARE SERVED, SO YOU CAN ENJOY A DINNER COMPRISING LOTS OF DIFFERENT DISHES.

Chilled almond and garlic soup
with grapes

A MOORISH TAKE ON GAZPACHO, whereby blanched almonds, garlic, and white bread take the place of fresh tomatoes and vegetables. A handful of grapes and toasted almonds added to each bowl contrasts and balances the delicate creaminess of the soup.

SERVES 4

7oz (200g) good rustic white bread
1 cup (150g) blanched almonds
1 large garlic clove, peeled and roughly chopped
generous ¾ cup (200ml) good-quality extra-virgin olive oil, plus extra to drizzle (optional)
1½–2 tbsp (20–30ml) sherry vinegar
1½–1¾ cups (350–400ml) ice-cold water

To serve:
5–7oz (150–200g) white seedless grapes, halved
2 tbsp (30ml) slivered or nibbed almonds, toasted
handful of ice cubes (optional)

Remove the crusts from the bread, then cut it into cubes and place in a bowl. Pour over enough cold water to just cover, let soak for 2 to 3 minutes, then squeeze out the excess water from the bread.

Put the bread into a food processor or blender. Add the almonds, garlic, olive oil, and sherry vinegar and blend until smooth. With the motor running, slowly pour in the ice-cold water until the soup is the thickness of heavy cream. If you prefer it thinner, add a little more water. Pour the soup into a bowl, cover, and refrigerate until well chilled.

To serve, ladle the soup into chilled bowls and arrange the halved grapes and toasted almonds on top. If you wish, add an ice cube to each bowl and drizzle over a little extra-virgin olive oil before serving.

Garlic **shrimp**

OF CATALAN ORIGIN, THIS SIMPLE TAPAS dish is now served all over Spain. Use very fresh shrimp to ensure a sweet, succulent result. Eat them with your fingers and don't forget to provide a bowl for the empty shrimp shells and individual bowls of lemon water for rinsing sticky fingers.

SERVES 4

1¹/₃lb (600g) large raw shrimp
4 tbsp (60ml) olive oil
5–6 garlic cloves, peeled and
    thinly sliced
2 dried red chiles, minced
sea salt and black pepper

To serve:
a few Italian parsley leaves,
    chopped
lemon wedges

Either leave the shrimp in their shells, or if you prefer, remove the heads, peel, and devein, leaving the tails intact.

Heat the olive oil in a large skillet. Add the garlic, dried chiles, and a pinch each of salt and pepper. Sauté over medium-low heat for about a minute until the garlic begins to color very slightly. Immediately tip the shrimp into the pan, increase the heat and cook for about 1¹/₂ minutes on each side until bright red and opaque.

Arrange the shrimp on a warm platter or individual plates, drizzle over the garlic-infused oil from the skillet, and sprinkle with a little chopped parsley. Serve immediately, with lemon wedges. Accompany with plenty of crusty bread.

Fava beans
with Iberico **ham**

THIS IS A CLASSIC SPANISH COMBINATION and one of the easiest tapas to assemble. I recommend using Iberico ham as its superb, slightly nutty flavor is second to none—you should be able to get it from a good deli.

SERVES 4

1lb (500g) fava beans (ideally freshly podded, otherwise frozen and thawed)
sea salt and black pepper
3 tbsp (45ml) olive oil
3¹/₂oz (100g) Iberico ham, diced
1 onion, peeled and minced
2 garlic cloves, peeled and minced
1 tbsp (15ml) chopped Italian parsley

Add the fava beans to a pan of boiling salted water, bring back to a boil, and blanch for 2 to 3 minutes until only just tender. Drain in a colander and place under cold running water to refresh, then drain again.

Heat the olive oil in a skillet. Add the ham and cook, stirring, for 2 to 3 minutes. Add the onion and garlic and cook gently for 6 to 8 minutes until softened but not colored. Tip the blanched fava beans into the skillet and toss over the heat for 2 to 3 minutes, seasoning well with salt and pepper to taste.

Transfer the fava beans and ham to a warm bowl, sprinkle with chopped parsley, and accompany with toasted slices of rustic bread.

Tortilla

THE RENOWNED TORTILLA HAS ATTAINED the title of national dish—the *tortilla Española*. Different kinds of tortilla exist all over Spain—in Valencia they are often made with rice and ham, whereas in Granada the popular *tortilla del Sacromonte* is made with bull's testicles and cow's brains. The following simple recipe is based on a typical Madrid-style tortilla.

SERVES 8

2lb (900g) medium mealy potatoes, such as Russet
generous ⅓ cup (100ml) olive oil
1 large onion, peeled and thinly sliced
sea salt and black pepper
6 large eggs

Peel the potatoes and cut them into thin slices. Heat the olive oil in a large, wide heavy pan. Add the potatoes and onion with some seasoning and toss well to coat in the oil. Reduce the heat and cook the potatoes for 15 to 20 minutes, stirring occasionally to prevent them from sticking to the bottom of the pan.

When the potatoes and onions are soft but not browned, remove the pan from the heat and drain off the excess oil into a bowl; save this for later. Whisk the eggs lightly in a large bowl; do not overbeat. Fold the slightly cooled potatoes into the egg mixture and let rest for a few minutes.

Heat 2–3 tbsp (30–45ml) of the reserved oil in a 10–10½-inch (25–26cm) nonstick skillet and pour in the potato and egg mixture, tilting the skillet to spread it evenly over the bottom. Let cook gently for 4 to 6 minutes or until the base is a light golden brown color and the tortilla begins to leave the sides of the skillet.

Carefully flip the tortilla over and cook the other side. To do this, run a flexible heatproof spatula around the sides of the tortilla, then place an inverted plate on top of the skillet and carefully turn both the skillet and plate over. Using the spatula, slide the tortilla back into the skillet so that the browned side is facing upward. Cook for a few more minutes until the underside is cooked; allow less time if you prefer the middle to be moist and slightly runny.

Carefully slide the tortilla onto a serving plate and allow to cool—it is best eaten at room temperature. Serve cut into wedges as a tapa, or alongside a mixed salad for a tasty lunch.

Paella with **chicken** and **chorizo**

ORIGINALLY FROM VALENCIA, paella is now cooked in every region of Spain. There are hundreds of different recipes, using just about any ingredient that works well with rice. *Paella Valenciana* traditionally includes chicken, rabbit, and snails, whereas *paella marisco* (mixed seafood paella) is more common in the coastal areas. Do try to buy a proper paella rice, as it will soak up more of the saffron-infused stock than long-grain rice.

SERVES 4–6

2¼ cups (400g) medium-grain paella rice, such as Bomba or Calasparra
6 boneless, skinless chicken thighs, about 1⅓lb (600g)
sea salt and black pepper
9oz (250g) raw chorizo sausage, skinned
3 tbsp (45ml) olive oil
1 red bell pepper, cored, seeded, and chopped
1 green bell pepper, cored, seeded, and chopped
6 garlic cloves, peeled and minced
½ cup (125ml) dry white wine
4 cups (1 liter) chicken stock
pinch of saffron strands
½ tsp (2ml) paprika
scant 1 cup (100g) peas, thawed if frozen
6 large tomatoes, skinned, seeded, and chopped
handful of Italian parsley leaves, chopped
lemon wedges, to serve

Rinse the rice well, drain, and set aside. Cut the chicken into bite-size pieces and season with salt and pepper. Cut the chorizo sausage into thick slices.

Heat the olive oil in a large sauté pan—or a paella pan if you have one—and brown the chicken pieces all over; remove to a plate and set aside. Add the chorizo slices to the pan and sauté for 2 minutes, then add the chopped peppers and garlic. Cook for 3 to 4 minutes, stirring frequently, until the peppers start to soften.

Stir in the rice and cook, stirring, for a few minutes to toast the grains. Pour in the wine and let it bubble until reduced by half. Now add the stock, saffron, and paprika. Bring to a boil, then return the chicken pieces to the pan and lower the heat. Simmer for 15 minutes, stirring every so often.

Add the peas and chopped tomatoes and continue cooking, very gently, for another 10 minutes, stirring every once in a while. When the rice is just cooked but still retains a slight bite, remove the pan from the heat and let stand for a few minutes.

Scatter the chopped parsley over the paella, then bring to the table and serve with lemon wedges.

Basque hake
and **potato** casserole

KNOWN AS MERLUZA, Basque hake is a dark-skinned fish with very tasty, firm flesh. It is considered a delicacy locally and can be quite expensive when caught from the Bay of Biscay. Merluza has become increasingly scarce so when I make this dish at home, I use the more sustainable South African Cape hake.

SERVES 4

1¹/₂lb (750g) hake fillets
4 garlic cloves, peeled
5 tbsp (75ml) olive oil
1 tbsp (15ml) sweet paprika
¹/₂ cup (125ml) dry white wine
1 large onion, peeled and thinly
   sliced
1lb (500g) new potatoes, peeled
   and quartered
sea salt and black pepper
1²/₃ cups (200g) peas, thawed if
   frozen

Check the hake for small bones, removing any with kitchen tweezers, then cut the fish into 2-inch (5cm) pieces and set aside. Thinly slice two of the garlic cloves. Heat 3 tbsp (45ml) olive oil in a skillet, add the sliced garlic, and cook gently until lightly golden. Remove from the heat and let the oil cool slightly before stirring in the paprika, followed by the wine. Set aside to infuse while you prepare the rest of the dish.

Cut the remaining 2 garlic cloves into quarters. Put the onion, potatoes, garlic quarters, and remaining olive oil into an ovenproof casserole. Add the garlic and paprika-infused wine and just enough water to cover. Season with salt and pepper and bring to a boil. Cook at a fast simmer for about 8 to 10 minutes, then add the hake pieces along with the peas. Lower the heat and cook at a gentle simmer for 3 to 5 minutes until both the potato and hake are just cooked. Taste and adjust the seasoning.

Ladle into warm bowls and serve at once, with plenty of rustic bread for mopping up the tasty juices.

Cod with romesco sauce

ROMESCO HAILS FROM CATALONIA, where it is frequently served as a sauce or a dip. Here, I'm baking cod fillets in a generous layer of romesco. It's a simple, healthy, and tasty way to cook any variety of white fish.

SERVES 4

4 thick cod fillets, with skin, about 6oz (175g) each
3 tbsp (45ml) olive oil
2/3 cup (100g) blanched almonds
3–4 garlic cloves, peeled and thinly sliced
1 onion, peeled and minced
pinch of dried red pepper flakes, to taste
6 ripe beef tomatoes, skinned and minced
1 bay leaf
sea salt and black pepper
3oz (85g) good-quality white bread (about 2 slices), toasted and roughly chopped
2 tbsp (30ml) chopped Italian parsley, plus extra to finish
3–4 tbsp (45–60ml) water
3 tbsp (45ml) sherry vinegar

Check the cod fillets for pin-bones and pull out any that you come across with kitchen tweezers. Chill until ready to cook.

Preheat the oven to 350°F (180°C). Heat the olive oil in a large skillet, add the almonds and garlic, and cook gently until lightly golden. Remove from the skillet with a slotted spoon and set aside on a plate.

Add the onion to the skillet and cook gently until lightly golden. Add the dried red pepper flakes, tomatoes, and bay leaf. Stir well and season with salt and pepper. Simmer for 10 minutes or so, until the tomatoes are soft.

Meanwhile, put the almonds and garlic, bread, and parsley into a blender or food processor with 1 tbsp (15ml) water. Blend to a rough paste and then stir into the tomato mixture, along with another 2–3 tbsp (30–45ml) water. Add the sherry vinegar, then taste and adjust the seasoning if necessary.

Arrange the cod fillets in an ovenproof dish, pour over the romesco sauce, cover the dish loosely with foil, and bake in the oven for 15 to 20 minutes, depending upon the thickness of the fish, until it is just done. Serve straight from the dish, sprinkled with a little chopped parsley.

Meatballs in tomato sauce

SPANISH MEATBALLS, OR *ALBONDIGAS*, are commonly
served as tapas in bars across Spain. They also make a fantastic main
course—served with steamed rice or eaten simply with rustic bread to
mop up the sauce.

SERVES 4–5

Spanish meatballs:

1lb (500g) good-quality ground
    beef
1 onion, peeled and very finely
    minced
1 garlic clove, peeled and minced
3/4 cup (50g) white bread crumbs
1oz (25g) Manchego (or cheddar),
    grated
2 tbsp (30ml) chopped Italian
    parsley, plus extra to finish
sea salt and black pepper
1 large egg, lightly beaten
2 tbsp (30ml) olive oil

Tomato sauce:

2 tbsp (30ml) olive oil
1 onion, peeled and very finely
    minced
1 garlic clove, peeled and minced
1/2 cup (120ml) dry white wine
2 x 14oz (400g) cans chopped
    tomatoes
generous 1/3 cup (100ml) water
1–2 tsp (5–10ml) superfine
    sugar

To make the meatballs, mix the ground beef, onion, garlic, bread crumbs,
cheese, and chopped parsley together in a large bowl until evenly
combined. Season well with salt and pepper and add the beaten egg
to bind, mixing with your hands. Break off a small piece of the mixture,
shape into a ball, and pan-fry in an oiled pan until cooked, then taste for
seasoning. Adjust the seasoning of the uncooked mixture as necessary.

With damp hands, shape the mixture into about 16 meatballs, trying not
to press them too tightly. Place on a large plate, cover with plastic wrap,
and chill for at least 30 minutes to allow them to firm up.

Meanwhile, make the tomato sauce. Heat the olive oil in a skillet, add the
onion and garlic, and cook gently until lightly golden. Increase the heat
slightly and pour in the wine. Let bubble until reduced by half, then stir
in the chopped tomatoes, water, and sugar. Season with salt and pepper.
Simmer for 10 to 15 minutes until the tomatoes are soft, then remove the
skillet from the heat.

To cook the meatballs, heat the olive oil in a large, wide pan. Add the
chilled meatballs and pan-fry for 5 minutes, turning frequently, until
browned all over. Pour the tomato sauce over them and simmer for
another 10 to 15 minutes until the meatballs are cooked through.

Divide the meatballs and tomato sauce between warm bowls and
sprinkle with chopped parsley to serve.

Orange caramel
sauce

Put the raw brown sugar into a dry, nonstick heavy pan and place over high heat. Swirl the pan to ensure that the sugar melts evenly. Once all of the sugar has dissolved and formed a golden brown caramel, carefully pour in the orange juice—take care as the mixture will splutter. Don't worry if the hot caramel seizes upon contact with the cold juice. Over gentle heat, swirl the pan frequently until the caramel has melted and the sauce is smooth. Take the pan off the heat.

Oranges in caramel
with sherry cream

THIS ELEGANT AND REFRESHING DESSERT is an ideal way to end a rich meal. For a smart finishing touch, I've added some candied orange zest, but you can omit this for a more straightforward dessert. If you do prepare the candied orange zests and have some left over, save them to decorate other desserts or cakes.

SERVES 4

6 oranges
generous 1/3 cup (75g) raw brown sugar
generous 1/3 cup (100ml) orange juice

Candied orange zest:
finely pared zest (in strips) from 3 of the above oranges
generous 1 cup (250ml) water
3/4 cup (150g) superfine sugar

Sherry cream:
1/4 cup (50ml) heavy cream
2 tbsp (30ml) confectioners' sugar, sifted
1–2 tbsp (15–30ml) medium sherry
few mint sprigs, to finish

To prepare the candied orange zest, remove any white pith from the zest strips, as this tastes very bitter, then slice the zest into thin strips. Pour the water into a small, heavy saucepan, add the superfine sugar, and dissolve over medium heat, stirring frequently. Add the orange zest, partially cover, and cook over medium-low heat for 40 to 50 minutes until tender. Set aside to allow the zest to cool in the syrup.

To prepare the oranges, cut off the base and top from each one (including the 3 zested fruit) and cut away all the peel and pith, following the curve of the fruit. Turn each orange on its side and cut into 1/2-inch (1cm) slices. Overlap the slices on individual serving plates and chill.

Now prepare the orange caramel sauce, following my guide (on the preceding pages). Let cool completely.

For the sherry cream, whip the cream with the confectioners' sugar in a large bowl until it begins to thicken. Flavor with the sherry to taste and continue to whip until the cream holds soft peaks. Cover and keep in the refrigerator until needed.

To serve, pour the cooled orange caramel sauce over the orange slices, then add a dollop of sherry cream. Scatter a little candied orange zest on top and finish with a sprig of mint. Serve at once.

Crema **Catalana**

SIMILAR TO THE FRENCH CRÈME BRÛLÉE
but with a softer, thinner consistency, this delectable dessert holds an important place in Catalan cuisine. Traditionally, it is prepared by the matriarch of the family and served only on St. Joseph's Day, March 19. Once tried, you may be tempted to make this creamy custard more than once a year.

SERVES 4–5

4 large egg yolks
generous 1/3 cup (70g) superfine sugar
2 tbsp (30ml) cornstarch, sifted
finely grated zest of 1 lemon
finely grated zest of 1 orange
1 cinnamon stick
generous 1 cup (250ml) whole milk
generous 1 cup (250ml) heavy cream
raw brown sugar, to sprinkle

In a large bowl, whisk the egg yolks and superfine sugar together until the mixture is pale and creamy. Whisk in the cornstarch and lemon and orange zests, then add the cinnamon stick. Now slowly pour in the milk and cream, whisking continuously.

Transfer the mixture to a heavy saucepan and cook over low heat, stirring constantly with a wooden spoon until the custard thickens enough to thickly coat the back of the spoon. At this stage, you should be able to feel some resistance as you stir the mixture. Do not overheat or it may curdle.

Remove from the heat and strain the custard through a fine strainer into a pitcher. Pour the custard into 4 or 5 ramekins, depending on size. Allow to cool completely, then transfer to the refrigerator and chill until needed.

Just before you are ready to serve, sprinkle a thin layer of raw brown sugar over the surface of each custard. Caramelize the sugar by waving a cook's blowtorch over the surface. (If you don't have a blowtorch, place the ramekins on a baking sheet under a preheated very hot broiler until the sugar is golden brown.) Either way, take care not to overheat the custards. Serve immediately.

BRITISH

SADLY, TRADITIONAL BRITISH FOOD HASN'T ENJOYED
A GREAT REPUTATION OVER THE YEARS, AS OTHER
"MORE EXCITING" CUISINES HAVE COME TO THE FORE.
RECENTLY, HOWEVER, SOME VERY TALENTED CHEFS
HAVE FOCUSED ON THE UK'S FOOD HERITAGE AND
HELPED TO PUT BRITISH FOOD BACK ONTO MENUS.
I'VE TRIED TO HELP THE MOVEMENT BY SERVING ONLY
BRITISH FOOD IN MY PUBS AND THE FEEDBACK HAS
BEEN AMAZING. WE HAVE SOME OF THE BEST PRODUCE
IN THE WORLD—WE JUST NEED TO VALUE IT AND MAKE
THE MOST OF IT. HOPEFULLY, VISITORS TO THE UK
WILL APPRECIATE THAT THERE'S MUCH MORE TO OUR
FOOD CULTURE THAN FISH 'N' CHIPS!

Celery and **Stilton soup**
with Stilton toasts

IDEAL FOR USING UP STILTON after Christmas, this soup is a great winter warmer. It is substantial enough to serve as a lunch, with the Stilton toasts, and perhaps a chicory, walnut, and clementine salad on the side.

SERVES 4

1 tbsp (15ml) butter
1 tbsp (15ml) olive oil
2 heads of celery, about 1$\frac{1}{2}$lb (700g), trimmed and chopped
1 onion, peeled and chopped
sea salt and black pepper
3$\frac{1}{3}$ cups (800ml) hot vegetable or chicken stock
3$\frac{1}{2}$oz (100g) Stilton, crumbled

Stilton toasts:
2oz (60g) Stilton, crumbled
2 tbsp (30ml) crème fraîche
handful of Italian parsley, leaves chopped
2 slices of brown bread, crusts removed

Heat the butter and olive oil in a medium saucepan. Add the celery, onion, and some seasoning and cook for 8 to 10 minutes, stirring frequently, until the vegetables are tender. Pour in just enough stock to cover and simmer for 3 to 5 minutes. Remove from the heat and let cool slightly.

Purée the soup using a free-standing blender, in batches if necessary, adding the Stilton as you go. Return the soup to the pan. Taste and adjust the seasoning if necessary.

For the Stilton toasts, preheat the broiler to high. In a small bowl, mix the Stilton, crème fraîche, and chopped parsley together and season lightly with salt and a good grinding of pepper. Lightly toast the bread on both sides. Spread with the Stilton mix and place under the broiler until the cheese is melted and bubbling. Cut each slice in half diagonally.

Reheat the soup, ladle into warm serving bowls, and grind over some pepper. Serve with the Stilton toasts on the side.

Warm **smoked salmon** and **watercress** salad

YOU CAN ASSEMBLE THIS LOVELY SALAD in minutes and enjoy it all year round. The hot-smoked salmon can be substituted with smoked trout or even peppery smoked mackerel if you like. When in season, use flavorful new potatoes for a real British treat.

SERVES 4–6

1lb (500g) baby new potatoes, scrubbed
sea salt
10oz (300g) hot smoked salmon
1/2 red onion, peeled and very thinly sliced
handful of dill, leaves roughly chopped
7oz (200g) young, tender watercress

Dressing:
2 tbsp (30ml) whisky
4 tsp (20ml) white wine vinegar
4 tsp (20ml) runny honey
4 tsp (20ml) grainy mustard
3 tbsp (45ml) peanut oil
3 tbsp (45ml) olive oil
sea salt and black pepper

Add the new potatoes to a pan of salted water, bring to a boil, and cook for 8 to 10 minutes until tender when pierced with a knife.

While the potatoes are cooking, prepare the dressing. Put the whisky, wine vinegar, honey, mustard, olive, and peanut oils in a small screw-topped jar, seal, and shake vigorously to combine. Season with salt and pepper to taste and set aside.

Drain the potatoes and place in a large bowl. Flake the salmon into bite-size pieces and add to the bowl along with the red onion and dill. Drizzle over some of the dressing and toss to coat.

Spread the potato and salmon mixture over a large platter, then scatter over the watercress. Drizzle with the remaining dressing and serve.

Baked egg and wild mushrooms

WILD MUSHROOMS TRANSFORM SIMPLE BAKED EGGS into a sophisticated appetizer. Serve with freshly made soda bread or hot buttered toast. This dish is also perfect for brunch, if you serve two eggs per person and increase the quantities of the other ingredients slightly.

SERVES 4

4 tsp (20ml) butter, plus extra for greasing
14oz (400g) wild mushrooms, cleaned and sliced
2 large shallots, peeled and minced
few thyme sprigs, leaves picked
sea salt and black pepper
4 large eggs
4 tbsp (60ml) heavy cream
1oz (25g) sharp cheddar, grated

Place a skillet over high heat. Add the butter and when it begins to foam, toss the wild mushrooms, shallots, and thyme leaves into the skillet. Season with salt and pepper. Cook, stirring frequently, for 3 to 5 minutes.

Preheat the oven to 375°F (190°C). Lightly butter 4 individual gratin dishes and divide the mushroom mixture between them. Make a well in the center and then carefully crack an egg into the well. Drizzle the cream around each egg and top with a sprinkling of grated cheese. Sprinkle with a pinch of salt and grind over some pepper.

Place the gratin dishes on a baking sheet and slide into the oven. Bake for 10 to 12 minutes for a runny yolk, or a couple of minutes longer if you prefer the yolk set. Serve at once, with soda bread or hot buttered toast.

Fish pie
with leeks and shrimp

A GOLDEN POTATO-TOPPED FISH PIE is always a winner, especially during the colder months. I generally add a couple of egg yolks to the mash as they help to set the potato topping and give it a lovely shine.

SERVES 6

1 onion, peeled and quartered
3–4 cloves
1 bay leaf
1 cup (250ml) heavy cream
1 cup (250ml) whole milk
14oz (400g) firm white fish fillets
14oz (400g) smoked haddock fillets (finnan haddie)
2 tbsp (30ml) butter
2 leeks, trimmed, well washed and thinly sliced
2 tbsp (30ml) all-purpose flour
sea salt and black pepper
handful of Italian parsley, leaves chopped
10oz (300g) peeled raw shrimp

Topping:
1¹/₂lb (750g) Desirée potatoes, peeled
¹/₃ cup (75g) butter, cubed
¹/₄ cup (50ml) hot milk
2 large egg yolks
3oz (85g) medium cheddar, grated

Stud the onion with the cloves. Put into a wide pan along with the bay leaf, cream, and milk and bring to a simmer. Lower the white and smoked fish fillets into the pan and poach for 3 to 4 minutes; it won't matter if the fish is slightly underdone at this stage. Lift it out of the pan onto a plate. Pass the cooking liquor through a fine strainer into a pitcher and reserve.

Melt the butter in a saucepan, add the leeks, and sweat for 4 to 6 minutes until soft. Stir in the flour and cook, stirring, for another couple of minutes. Gradually stir in the reserved fish cooking liquor and let simmer for 10 to 15 minutes, stirring from time to time, until thickened to a sauce consistency. Season well with salt and pepper to taste and stir in the chopped parsley.

For the topping, cut the potatoes into chunks and add to a pan of salted water. Bring to the boil, lower the heat, and cook for 15 to 20 minutes until tender when pierced with a knife. Drain well and push through a potato ricer, or mash until smooth. Add the butter and hot milk and mix until well incorporated. Allow to cool slightly, then stir in the egg yolks. Season well.

Preheat the oven to 400°F (200°C). Flake the fish into bite-size pieces and add to the leek sauce with the shrimp. Stir until evenly combined. Transfer to a 7–8-cup (1.75–2 liter) ovenproof baking dish and spoon the mash on top, spreading it evenly. For a traditional finish, mark the surface with the tines of a fork. Scatter over a generous layer of grated cheese. Bake in the oven for 25 to 30 minutes until the pie is bubbling and golden brown on top. Let stand for a few minutes, then serve with peas or green beans.

Lamb rib roast
with samphire

LAMB AND SEA-SALTY SAMPHIRE are perfect partners for a summer roast. Samphire has a short season, peaking in July in the UK. It is available from fish suppliers, as well as markets and selected supermarkets. When you can't get hold of any, serve the lamb racks with braised fennel or a simple watercress salad instead.

SERVES 4

2 lamb rib roast (rack of lamb), with 6 bones each
sea salt and black pepper
2 tbsp (30ml) olive oil
7oz (200g) samphire
1 tbsp (25ml) butter
2–3 anchovy fillets, roughly chopped
grated zest and juice of 1/2 lemon
1/3 cup (50g) hazelnuts, halved and toasted

Preheat the oven to 400°F (200°C). Season the lamb rib roasts with salt and pepper. Heat the olive oil in a large ovenproof pan or roasting tray and brown the lamb rib roasts, fat-side down, for 2 to 3 minutes. Turn the roasts fat side uppermost and transfer to the oven. Roast for 15 minutes for medium-rare meat, or 20 minutes for medium. Remove from the oven, cover loosely with foil, and let rest in a warm place for at least 10 minutes.

Meanwhile, bring a large pan of salted water to a boil. Add the samphire and cook for 2 to 3 minutes until just tender. Refresh in a bowl of ice water, then drain again.

When you are almost ready to serve, melt the butter in a large skillet over medium-high heat. As it begins to foam, add the anchovy fillets, samphire, and lemon zest and juice. Warm through for 2 to 3 minutes, then add the toasted hazelnuts and a generous grinding of pepper.

To serve, divide the samphire between warm plates. Carve the lamb rib roasts into individual chops and arrange on top of the samphire. Spoon over any pan juices from the samphire and lamb. Serve immediately, with new potatoes or a fluffy mash.

Pheasant casserole with winter vegetables and colcannon

THIS RUSTIC CASSEROLE TASTES EVEN BETTER the day after it has been made. Just be sure to reheat it gently so that the pheasant meat remains moist and succulent. Irish colcannon—creamy mash with shredded cabbage—makes a lovely accompaniment, but you could serve the casserole with ordinary mash and braised red cabbage if you prefer.

SERVES 6–8

2 pheasants, about 1lb 4oz (550g) each
1 tbsp (15ml) all-purpose flour
sea salt and black pepper
3 tbsp (45ml) olive oil
7oz (200g) smoked bacon, cut into cubes
2 carrots, peeled and thickly sliced
2 large parsnips, peeled and cut into chunks
1/2 celeriac (celery root), peeled and cut into chunks
12 pearl onions, peeled
2 tbsp (30ml) runny honey
generous 3/4 cup (200ml) red wine
few thyme sprigs
2 cups (500ml) chicken stock

Colcannon:
1 1/2lb (750g) mealy potatoes, such as Russet
1/2 savoy cabbage, trimmed
generous 1/3 cup (80g) butter, cut into cubes
5 tbsp (75ml) heavy cream, warmed

Preheat the oven to 350°F (180°C). Joint the pheasants. Season the flour with salt and pepper and use to lightly dust the pheasant pieces. Heat the olive oil in a large ovenproof casserole and brown the pheasant pieces all over, in batches if necessary. Set aside on a plate.

Add the bacon cubes to the casserole and cook for 2 to 3 minutes, stirring frequently. Add the carrots, parsnips, celeriac, and pearl onions to the pan and cook, stirring, for 2 to 3 minutes until starting to soften. Add the honey, pour in the wine, and cook until the liquid has reduced by half. Return the pheasants to the casserole, add the thyme, and pour over the stock. Season with salt and pepper, put the lid on the casserole, and place in the oven. Cook for 1 to 1 1/4 hours until the meat is tender.

Make the colcannon while the casserole is in the oven. Peel the potatoes and cut them into large, even-size chunks. Add to a pan of salted water, bring to a boil, and cook for 12 to 15 minutes until tender. Meanwhile, finely shred the cabbage. Place a skillet over medium heat and add a quarter of the butter. When it has melted, add the cabbage and sauté gently for 4 to 6 minutes until tender. Remove from the heat and set aside.

Drain the potatoes well, then return to the pan and place over low heat to dry out for a minute. Take off the heat and pass through a potato ricer back into the pan, or mash well. Slowly stir in the cream, season well, and gradually beat in the rest of the butter. Stir the cabbage through the mashed potato and check the seasoning.

Divide the pheasant casserole between warm plates and serve each portion with a generous helping of colcannon.

Ham with pease pudding and parsley sauce

HEARTY, SIMPLE, AND SATISFYING, boiled ham and pease pudding makes a great weekday supper or casual Sunday lunch. A classic parsley sauce finishes the dish perfectly. You'll just need to remember to put the ham to soak the night before in plenty of cold water to remove excess salt.

SERVES 4

4lb (2kg) boneless smoked ham
   joint, soaked (see above)
1 onion, peeled and quartered
1 carrot, peeled and quartered
2 celery stalks, cut into chunks
2 bay leaves
few thyme sprigs
1 tsp (5ml) black peppercorns

Pease pudding:

1lb (500g) yellow split peas,
   soaked overnight in cold water
1 onion, peeled and quartered
1 carrot, peeled and quartered
2 bay leaves
2 tbsp (30ml) malt vinegar
sea salt and white pepper
4 tsp (20ml) butter, cut into cubes

Parsley sauce:

4 tsp (20ml) butter
2 shallots, peeled and finely diced
$1^{1}/_{2}$ tbsp (20ml) all-purpose flour
$1^{1}/_{2}$ tsp (7.5ml) English mustard
$^{2}/_{3}$ cup (150ml) whole milk
handful of Italian parsley,
   leaves chopped
1 tbsp (15ml) heavy cream
lemon juice, to taste

Drain the ham and place in a large saucepan with the onion, carrot, celery, bay leaves, thyme, and black peppercorns. Pour on enough water to cover, then bring to a boil. Skim off any scum that rises to the surface. Lower the heat and simmer gently for about 2 hours, skimming occasionally, until the ham is cooked through. Leave in the liquor.

For the pease pudding, drain the soaked peas and tip into a saucepan. Add the onion, carrot, and bay leaves and cover with water (adding some of the stock from the ham if it's not too salty). Bring to a boil and skim off any scum that rises to the surface. Lower the heat and simmer gently for an hour or until the peas are tender.

Discard the onion, carrot, and bay leaves and tip the peas into a blender. Blitz to a purée, then pour into a clean pan. Add the vinegar and season with salt and pepper. Gradually beat in the butter, a cube at a time. Keep warm until ready to serve, adding a little water if it becomes too dry.

To make the parsley sauce, melt the butter in a small saucepan, add the shallots, and sauté gently until softened but not colored, 4 to 6 minutes. Add the flour and mustard, stir well, and cook for another 2 to 3 minutes. Gradually stir in the milk and $^{2}/_{3}$ cup (150ml) strained liquor from the ham. Bring to a boil, lower the heat, and simmer for 6 to 8 minutes, stirring every so often. The sauce should be quite thick.

Just before serving, stir the chopped parsley, cream, and a squeeze of lemon juice into the sauce and check the seasoning. Lift the ham out of the liquor onto a board. Carve the meat into thick slices and warm through in some of the liquor if necessary. Serve with the pease pudding and parsley sauce.

5 ways with asparagus

Asparagus with **lemon** and **tarragon hollandaise**

For the hollandaise, cut scant $1/2$ cup (100g) chilled unsalted butter into small cubes. Beat 2 large egg yolks with a squeeze of lemon juice, a cube of butter, and some seasoning in a bowl set over a pan of simmering water until very thick and creamy. Beat in the rest of the butter, a cube at a time, then continue to beat until the hollandaise is shiny and thick. Season with sea salt, black pepper, and lemon juice to taste and fold in some freshly chopped tarragon leaves. Blanch 1lb (450g) trimmed asparagus in boiling salted water for 2 to 3 minutes until tender. Drain well and serve with the hollandaise. **SERVES 4**

Boiled **egg** and **asparagus** soldiers

Heat the oven to 400°F (200°C). Cut 8 prosciutto slices in half and wrap a half-slice around each of 16 asparagus spears. Lay on a lightly oiled baking sheet, drizzle with olive oil, and grind over some black pepper. Bake for 10 to 12 minutes until the ham is crisp and the asparagus is tender. Meanwhile, add 4 large eggs to a pan of boiling salted water and boil for 4 minutes. Remove and place each one in an eggcup. Serve the boiled eggs at once, on warm plates with the asparagus soldiers. **SERVES 4**

Shaved **asparagus** and **fennel salad**

Finely slice 8–10 trimmed asparagus spears on the diagonal using a mandolin. Slice 1 trimmed medium fennel bulb in the same manner. Combine in a large bowl. Mix the juice of $1/2$ lemon, $1/2$ tsp (2ml) Dijon mustard, 4 tbsp (60ml) extra-virgin olive oil, $1/2$ tsp (2ml) superfine sugar, and sea salt and black pepper to taste in a small bowl. Pour over the asparagus and fennel shavings and toss well. Cover and chill for at least 15 to 20 minutes. To serve, add about $3^1/2$oz (100g) tender watercress leaves, a handful of toasted pine nuts, and some Parmesan shavings to the salad and toss lightly. **SERVES 4**

Asparagus, bacon, and **goat cheese frittata**

Heat 1 tbsp (15ml) olive oil in a medium nonstick skillet over medium heat. Toss in generous $1/2$ cup (100g) diced bacon and cook until lightly golden. Stir in 1 minced garlic clove, 9oz (250g) roughly chopped trimmed asparagus, and some thyme leaves. Cook for 3 to 4 minutes until the asparagus is just tender. Meanwhile, beat 4 large eggs with 2–3 tbsp (30–45ml) cream, $1/4$ cup (20g) grated Parmesan, and plenty of seasoning. Pour the egg mixture into the skillet and stir gently to distribute the ingredients evenly. Scatter over $3^1/2$oz (100g) crumbled goat cheese. Cook over low heat, without stirring, until the eggs begin to set at the sides and on the bottom. Place the skillet under a hot broiler for 1 to 2 minutes until lightly set. Let stand for a minute before serving. **SERVES 2**

Asparagus and smoked **salmon tartlets**

Roll out 10oz (300g) short pie dough on a lightly floured counter to the thickness of $1/8$ inch (3mm) and use to line 6 tartlet pans. Chill for at least 30 minutes. Blanch 7oz (200g) trimmed asparagus in boiling salted water for 2 to 4 minutes until just tender. Drain, refresh in ice water, drain again, and cut into $1^1/4$-inch (3cm) lengths. Heat the oven to 400°F (200°C). Line the pastry shells with foil and dried beans and bake "blind" for 15 to 20 minutes. Remove the foil and beans; bake for another 5 minutes. Lower the oven to 375°F (190°C). In a bowl, lightly beat $2/3$ cup (150ml) heavy cream and 1 large egg with some sea salt and black pepper. Scatter 3oz (85g) flaked hot-smoked salmon in the pastry shells and arrange the asparagus on top. Spoon over the cream mixture, then sprinkle with scant $1/4$ cup (20g) grated cheddar. Bake for 10 to 15 minutes until golden and set. Let cool slightly. **SERVES 6**

Steamed marmalade
sponge **pudding**

A MOIST, STICKY STEAMED PUDDING IS DEEPLY COMFORTING and conjures up nostalgic childhood memories. Serve this one with a drizzle of pouring cream or custard, or—for an indulgent treat—clotted cream spiked with a little orange liqueur. If you have any on hand, top the pudding with candied orange zest (see page 102).

SERVES 4

scant ²/₃ cup (140g) butter, softened, plus extra for greasing
3 tbsp (45ml) marmalade
2 tbsp (30ml) corn syrup
finely grated zest of 1 orange
scant ³/₄ cup (140g) unrefined superfine sugar
3 large eggs, lightly beaten
¹/₂ cup (70g) self-rising flour
2 tsp (10ml) baking powder
2 tbsp (30ml) whole milk

Lightly butter a 5-cup (1.2 liter) ovenproof bowl. Mix 1 tbsp (15ml) of the marmalade with the corn syrup and orange zest and spread over the bottom of the ovenproof bowl.

Cream together the butter and sugar, using an electric mixer, until soft. With the motor still running, add the beaten eggs a little at a time, making sure each addition is fully incorporated before the next is added. Sift in the flour and baking powder and fold in alternately with the milk and remaining marmalade to obtain a smooth mixture. Spoon into the ovenproof bowl.

Lay a pleated buttered sheet of waxed paper on top of the bowl, buttered side down, and cover with a pleated sheet of foil, of the same size. Secure tightly with string under the rim of the bowl.

Stand the bowl on a trivet or upturned small heatproof plate in a large saucepan. Pour in enough boiling water to come halfway up the side of the bowl and bring to a steady simmer. Cover with a tight-fitting lid and steam for 1¹/₂ hours, checking the water level every 30 minutes or so, and topping off with boiling water as needed.

To check if the pudding is ready, unwrap and insert a skewer into the sponge; it should come out clean. Unmold the hot pudding onto a warm serving plate and serve, with cream or custard.

Strawberry shortbread stacks

STRAWBERRIES AND CREAM epitomize the British summer. Fold them together and serve between shortbread circles for a simple, yet elegant dessert. Homemade shortbread is unbeatable—you'll have more than you need for these stacks, but extras will keep well in an airtight tin for up to a week. If you are short of time, fine-quality bought shortbread will make this an almost instant dessert.

SERVES 4–6

Shortbread:
generous 1 cup (150g) all-purpose flour, plus extra to dust
$^3/_4$ cup (100g) rice flour
$^1/_2$ tsp (2ml) fine sea salt
$^1/_2$ cup (125g) unsalted butter, at room temperature
scant $^1/_2$ cup (90g) superfine sugar
1 large egg, beaten

Strawberry cream:
$^1/_4$ cup (50ml) heavy cream
$^2/_3$ cup (150g) clotted cream (Devonshire cream)
3–4 tbsp (45–60ml) confectioners' sugar, sifted, plus extra to dust
1 vanilla bean, slit open lengthwise
scant $3^1/_4$ cups (400g) strawberries, hulled and quartered or cut into wedges

To make the shortbread, sift the flour, rice flour, and salt together. Beat the butter and superfine sugar together, using an electric mixer, until smooth. Add the egg slowly, then turn the machine to its lowest setting and add the flour, a spoonful at a time, until the mixture just comes together and forms a soft dough; do not overwork. Press the dough into a ball, wrap in plastic wrap, and chill for at least an hour.

Meanwhile, for the strawberry cream, put the heavy cream, clotted cream, and confectioners' sugar into a bowl and scrape in the seeds from the vanilla bean, using the tip of a knife. Beat until the mixture is thick and forms soft peaks. Set aside until you are ready to assemble the dessert.

Preheat the oven to 325°F (160°C). On a lightly floured counter, roll out the dough to a $^1/_8$ inch (3–4mm) thickness and cut out circles, using a $3^1/_2$–4-inch (9–10cm) cookie cutter. Place the circles on a baking sheet and bake in the oven for 20 to 25 minutes until pale golden. Leave on the baking sheet for a couple of minutes to firm up, then transfer to a wire rack and let cool completely.

To serve, fold the strawberries through the vanilla cream, reserving a handful. Put a shortbread in the center of each plate and spoon the strawberry cream on top. Top with another shortbread circle, lightly dust with confectioners' sugar, and place the reserved strawberries alongside.

Making custard

Put the milk, cream, and 1 tbsp (15ml) of the superfine sugar into a heavy saucepan and slowly bring to a boil. Meanwhile, beat the egg yolks and the rest of the sugar together in a large bowl, using a hand whisk, until light and creamy. Just before the creamy milk comes to a boil, gradually pour it onto the egg and sugar mixture, whisking continuously. Strain the mixture through a fine strainer back into the pan and place over low heat. Stir constantly with a wooden spoon until the custard thickens enough to coat the back of the spoon; do not overheat or it will curdle. Remove from the heat and strain the custard through a fine strainer once more.

Rhubarb fool

BEAUTIFUL BRIGHT PINK, FORCED RHUBARB makes a delicious creamy fool. Lightly stew the fruit with vanilla and sugar, allow to cool, then marry with a delicate custard. The rhubarb stems break down easily when heated, so cook for less time if you prefer the fruit to hold its shape and have a firmer texture.

SERVES 4–6

1lb (500g) rhubarb
generous ⅓ cup (75g) soft light
    brown sugar
finely grated zest and juice of
    1 orange
1 vanilla bean, slit open

Custard:
⅔ cup (150ml) whole milk
generous 1 cup (250ml) heavy
    cream
¼ cup (50g) superfine sugar
6 large egg yolks

Cut the rhubarb stems into short lengths and place in a saucepan with the brown sugar, orange zest, and juice. Add a splash of water and scrape the seeds from the vanilla bean into the pan, using the tip of a knife. Place over high heat. When the liquid begins to bubble, lower the heat and simmer gently for 8 to 10 minutes or until the rhubarb is tender. Remove from the heat and allow to cool completely, then chill.

Now make the custard, following my guide (on the preceding pages). Pour into a chilled bowl and allow to cool, stirring every so often to prevent a skin from forming. Chill until needed.

When ready to serve, lightly fold two-thirds of the chilled rhubarb through the chilled custard. Drop a small spoonful of rhubarb into each serving glass, then top with the rippled fool. Spoon the remaining rhubarb on top and serve straightaway.

MIDDLE EASTERN

FROM A CULINARY PERSPECTIVE, THE MIDDLE EAST ENCOMPASSES COUNTRIES FROM AS FAR AS ALGERIA AND MOROCCO IN THE WEST TO OMAN AND IRAN IN THE EAST. THE VARIETY OF RESTAURANTS IN THE UK HAVE GIVEN US A TASTE FOR AROMATIC NORTH AFRICAN TAGINES AS WELL AS PERSIAN FOOD—RICH WITH HERBS, SPICES, AND FRUIT. AND IT'S NO LONGER DIFFICULT TO SOURCE INGREDIENTS FOR A MIDDLE EASTERN MEAL. I PARTICULARLY LOVE THE MEZE CONCEPT OF SHARING A RANGE OF DISHES AT THE START OF A MEAL—A CUSTOM THAT HELPS TO BRING FAMILY AND FRIENDS TOGETHER THROUGH FOOD.

Zucchini, feta, and **herb** fritters

THESE TASTY VEGETARIAN FRITTERS are ideal as a light appetizer or as part of a meze spread. To prepare ahead, cook the fritters in advance and reheat them in a low oven when ready to serve.

SERVES 5–6

3 medium or 2 large zucchini, about 1lb (500g)
sea salt and black pepper
2 tbsp (30ml) light olive oil, plus extra to cook the fritters
1 large onion, peeled and thinly sliced
3 large eggs
7oz (200g) feta, diced
small handful of mint sprigs, leaves chopped
small handful of dill sprigs, leaves chopped
2 tbsp (30ml) pine nuts
3–4 tbsp (45–60ml) all-purpose flour

To serve:
lemon wedges
Italian parsley sprigs (optional)

Trim the zucchini and coarsely grate them into a strainer set on top of a bowl. Sprinkle over a pinch of salt, mix well, and let stand for about 10 minutes. (The salt will help to draw out excess moisture.) Squeeze the grated zucchini with your hands to remove some of the juices, then tip into a large bowl.

Meanwhile, heat 2 tbsp (30ml) olive oil in a wide skillet and sauté the onion, with a pinch each of salt and pepper, for 5 to 6 minutes until softened. Let cool slightly, then add to the zucchini and mix well.

Add the eggs, feta, chopped herbs, pine nuts, and 3 tbsp (45ml) flour to the zucchini mixture. Add a generous grinding of pepper and mix well until evenly combined. (As the feta is salty, you probably won't need to add salt.) If the batter seems too wet, add another 1 tbsp (15ml) flour and mix well.

Heat a thin layer of olive oil in a wide skillet. You will need to cook the fritters in batches: drop several spoonfuls of the batter into the skillet, spacing them apart, and cook for 2 to 3 minutes on each side until golden brown. Transfer to a warm plate lined with paper towels and keep warm while you cook the rest; there should be enough for 20–24 small fritters.

Serve the zucchini fritters warm, with lemon wedges and a parsley garnish, if you like.

Shaping dolmades

Lay a grape leaf, shiny-side down, on a clean counter. Place a heaping teaspoonful (5ml) of the filling in the middle of the leaf, nearer to the stem edge. Fold over the stem end to cover the filling, then tuck in both sides of the grape leaf and roll up like a cigar. Repeat with the remaining grape leaves and filling.

Dolmades

THESE STUFFED GRAPE LEAVES ARE NOT DIFFICULT to make, but rolling them does take time, particularly as I usually double the recipe to feed a crowd. I try to make it a family affair and enlist the kids' help—the best way to persuade them that something is really good to eat. If you are cooking the rice from scratch, you'll need about 1 cup (200g) uncooked weight.

SERVES 4

7¹/₂oz (230g) package grape leaves in brine
2 tbsp (30ml) olive oil, plus extra to drizzle
1 large onion, peeled and minced
2 garlic cloves, peeled and minced
2¹/₄ cups (400g) cooked white rice, preferably long-grain
scant 1 cup (100g) pine nuts, toasted
¹/₂ cup (100g) golden raisins
¹/₄ tsp (1ml) ground allspice
¹/₂ tsp (2ml) ground cinnamon
pinch of superfine sugar
2 ripe tomatoes, skinned, seeded, and chopped
small handful of Italian parsley, chopped
small handful of mint, chopped
sea salt and black pepper
about 1¹/₄ cups (300ml) vegetable stock
juice of ¹/₂ lemon, plus extra to drizzle
extra-virgin olive oil, to drizzle

Baba ganoush (top); dolmades (left); tabbouleh (right)

To remove excess salt from the grape leaves, put them into a large bowl, and pour on boiling water to cover. Let soak for a few minutes, then carefully drain off the liquid. Rinse under cold water and drain again.

Heat the olive oil in a pan and gently cook the onion and garlic for a few minutes, stirring occasionally, until softened. Tip into a bowl and add the cooked rice, pine nuts, golden raisins, allspice, cinnamon, sugar, tomatoes, herbs, and seasoning. Taste and adjust the seasoning (as the dolmades will be served cold, you need to season generously).

Now stuff the grape leaves with the rice filling, following my guide (on the preceding pages).

Drape a clean, wet dish towel in a wide pan to lie flat on the bottom, with the sides overhanging the edge of the pan. Pack the grape leaves on top in tight, neat layers. Add the stock, lemon juice, and a drizzle of olive oil.

Cover the dolmades with a piece of baking parchment, and then place a small heatproof plate that just fits inside the pan on top. (This will prevent the dolmades from unwrapping during cooking.) Cover the pan with a lid and simmer gently for an hour.

Remove the plate and then carefully take the dolmades out of the pan by lifting the dish towel. Transfer to a tray and let cool. Chill for a few hours, or overnight if preparing ahead. Take the dolmades out of the refrigerator 10 minutes before serving. Drizzle with a little extra-virgin olive oil and lemon juice to serve.

Baba ganoush

FROM THE LEVANT THROUGH TO TURKEY AND EGYPT, this lovely eggplant dip is popular throughout the Middle East. Naturally, there are slight variations on the seasoning and ingredients used, depending on where you are. The eggplants can either be roasted or grilled over an open flame until the flesh is soft and smoky. Prepare the dip in advance and serve at room temperature.

SERVES 4–6

2 large eggplants, about
   1^1/$_3$lb (600–650g)
a little oil, for oiling
juice of ^{1}/$_2$ lemon, or to taste
4 tsp (20ml) tahini (sesame seed
   paste)
2 tbsp (30ml) plain yogurt
2 fat garlic cloves, peeled and
   crushed
1 thyme sprig, leaves picked
sea salt and black pepper

To serve:
extra-virgin olive oil, to drizzle
few pinches of sumac, or a little
   chopped Italian parsley,
   to sprinkle

Preheat the oven to 425°F (220°C). Prick each eggplant several times with the tip of a sharp knife, then place both on a lightly oiled baking sheet. Roast in the hot oven for 45 to 60 minutes, turning them over halfway, until the skins are wrinkly and the eggplants feel soft when lightly pressed; they should almost collapse upon themselves.

Leave the eggplants until cool enough to handle, then peel away the blackened skins and put the flesh into a colander. Press with the back of a ladle to squeeze out as much liquid as possible, then tip the eggplant flesh onto a board and chop roughly (or blitz in a blender for a smooth texture if preferred).

Put the chopped eggplant into a bowl and add the lemon juice, tahini, yogurt, garlic, thyme leaves, and seasoning. Mix well, then taste and adjust the seasoning. (Cover and chill if not serving immediately.)

Spoon the baba ganoush into a serving bowl and drizzle a little extra-virgin olive oil over the surface. Sprinkle with a little sumac or chopped parsley to garnish and serve, with warm flat breads.

Illustrated on page 142

Tabbouleh

A GORGEOUS BULGUR WHEAT SALAD teeming with freshly chopped herbs, tomatoes, and green onions. Traditional tabbouleh recipes use fine ground bulgur wheat, which is available at delis and Middle Eastern grocers if you would prefer to use it. This salad is best mixed when you are about to serve it, as the lemon juice will discolor the herbs with time. Serve the dish as a meze or accompaniment to fish and meat dishes.

SERVES 4–6

scant ¹/₂ cup (75g) bulgur wheat
9oz (250g) ripe plum tomatoes
juice of 1 small lemon, or to taste
3 tbsp (45ml) extra-virgin olive oil
sea salt and black pepper
3 green onions, trimmed
bunch of Italian parsley, about 2³/₄oz (75g)
bunch of mint, about 2³/₄oz (75g)
seeds from ¹/₂ small pomegranate, to garnish
   (optional)

Put the bulgur wheat into a bowl, pour on boiling water to cover generously, then cover the bowl with plastic wrap and let the grains swell for 10 minutes. Tip the bulgur wheat into a fine strainer and drain very thoroughly, then return to the bowl.

Finely dice the tomatoes and add to the bulgur wheat, along with the lemon juice, extra-virgin olive oil, and some salt and pepper. Mix well, using a fork, and then let the bulgur soak up the juices and soften a little more. Taste and adjust the seasoning.

Meanwhile, mince the green onions and roughly shred the parsley and mint leaves with a sharp knife. When you are ready to serve, fold the herbs through the bulgur wheat and garnish with a scattering of pomegranate seeds, if you wish.

Illustrated on page 142

Pan-fried **red mullet** with **saffron pilaf** and **tarator** sauce

IN LEBANON AND TURKEY, LOCAL FISH are often pan-fried and served with tarator sauce and saffron rice. Here I'm serving red mullet fillets, but any firm white fish can be prepared in the same way. Save any leftover sauce to serve with broiled meat or poultry.

SERVES 4

4 red mullet, about 14oz (400g)
   each, filleted (skin on)
2 tbsp (30ml) all-purpose flour
1/2 tsp (2ml) ground cumin
1/2 tsp (2ml) ground ginger
1/2 tsp (2ml) ground cinnamon
sea salt and black pepper
2–3 tbsp (30–45ml) olive oil

Saffron rice pilaf:
4 tbsp (60ml) olive oil
2 large onions, peeled and finely
   sliced
1 1/2 cups (300g) long-grain rice
2 1/2 cups (600ml) hot chicken or
   vegetable stock
pinch of saffron strands
2/3 cup (75g) pine nuts, toasted
handful of Italian parsley, leaves
   chopped

Tarator sauce:
4 tbsp (60ml) tahini
1/2 cup (50g) pine nuts, toasted
3 tbsp (45ml) lemon juice, to taste
1 garlic clove, peeled and chopped
1/2 tsp (2ml) ground cumin
pinch of cayenne pepper
3–4 tbsp (45–60ml) hot water

Check the fish for small bones, removing any with kitchen tweezers. Set aside at room temperature while you prepare the pilaf.

For the saffron rice pilaf, heat half the olive oil in a medium heavy pan. Add the onions with a pinch each of salt and pepper and sauté for 5 to 6 minutes until starting to soften. Add the remaining oil and tip in the rice. Stir well and cook, stirring, for a minute, then add the stock and saffron. Bring to a simmer, cover with a tight-fitting lid, and cook for 8 to 10 minutes, just until most of the stock has been absorbed. Turn off the heat and let the rice steam in the covered pan for another 5 minutes.

While the rice is cooking, make the tarator sauce. Put the tahini, pine nuts, lemon juice, garlic, cumin, cayenne, and some seasoning into a food processor and blitz on high speed. With the machine running, add the water, 1 tbsp (15ml) at a time, until the sauce is smooth with the consistency of a light mayonnaise. Adjust the flavor to taste, with additional lemon juice or salt. Transfer to a serving bowl.

About 5 minutes before the rice will be ready, cook the fish. Season the flour with the cumin, ginger, cinnamon, and salt and pepper and use to coat the red mullet fillets. Heat the olive oil in a wide skillet until hot. Pan-fry the fillets for 1 1/2 to 2 minutes on each side until golden brown and just cooked through; the fish should feel just firm when pressed.

Serve the fish on the saffron rice with a generous spoonful of tarator sauce alongside. Scatter over the pine nuts and chopped parsley. Put the remaining sauce in a bowl on the table for guests to help themselves.

Lamb tagine with apricots and herb couscous

LAMB AND FRUIT GO WELL TOGETHER and this stew includes some tangy preserved lemons to balance out the sweetness of the dried fruit. When fresh apricots are in season, you can use 7oz (200g) of these instead: cut into wedges, discarding the pits, and add to the stew once the lamb is tender—they'll only need a few minutes to soften; you may need to add a little more honey, too.

SERVES 4

2lb (900g) boned lamb shoulder
2 tbsp (30ml) all-purpose flour
sea salt and black pepper
4 tbsp (60ml) olive oil
1 large onion, peeled and finely
    sliced
2 garlic cloves, peeled and
    crushed
1 tbsp (15ml) grated gingerroot
4 tsp (20ml) ras el hanout
    (Moroccan spice mix)
4 tsp (20ml) tomato paste
about 3¹/₃ cups (800ml) lamb or
    chicken stock
generous ¹/₂ cup (100g) dried
    apricots, chopped
1¹/₂ preserved lemons, chopped
squeeze of lemon juice
1–2 tbsp (15–30ml) runny honey

Herb couscous:
2 cups (500ml) chicken stock
1³/₄ cups (300g) couscous
large handful of Italian parsley
large handful of mint
small handful of cilantro
finely grated zest of 1 lemon
2 tsp (10ml) lemon juice
2 tbsp (30ml) extra-virgin olive oil

Cut the lamb into bite-size chunks. Season the flour with salt and pepper and toss the lamb in it to coat. Heat half the olive oil in a large heavy pan or ovenproof casserole and brown the meat in batches, turning to color all over and transferring to a plate once browned.

Add the onion and a little more oil to the pan, if necessary, and sauté for 5 minutes until it starts to soften. Add the garlic, gingerroot, ras el hanout, and tomato paste and cook for a few minutes until fragrant. Return the lamb and any juices to the pan and stir well.

Pour in enough stock to cover everything and bring to a boil, then reduce to a simmer. Skim the surface frequently until the stock is clear, then partially cover the pan with the lid and cook gently, stirring occasionally, for 1¹/₂ hours.

Stir in the apricots, preserved lemons, lemon juice, and honey to taste. Simmer, uncovered, for another 30 to 45 minutes, stirring frequently, until the lamb is tender. Taste and adjust the seasoning. (The stew can be prepared ahead and reheated before serving, if more convenient.)

To make the couscous, bring the stock to a boil. Tip the couscous into a large bowl, then pour on the stock. Cover the bowl with plastic wrap and leave for 10 to 15 minutes until all the stock has been absorbed. Meanwhile, strip the herb leaves from their stalks and chop them.

Fluff up the couscous with a fork to separate the grains, then fork through the herbs, lemon zest, and some seasoning. Mix the lemon juice and extra-virgin olive oil together, then fork through the couscous and check the seasoning. Serve with the lamb tagine.

Turkish yogurt cake with citrus syrup

THIS MOIST, DENSE YOGURT CAKE has a similar texture to a light cheesecake. The citrus syrup gives the top a lovely sheen and imparts a tangy sweetness. Save any leftover syrup to drizzle over cold vanilla ice cream, plain yogurt, or breakfast crêpes.

SERVES 8

butter, for greasing
6 large eggs, separated
3/4 cup (150g) superfine sugar
1/2 cup (75g) self-rising flour
2 1/2 cups (600g) strained plain
    Greek yogurt
finely grated zest and juice of
    1 lemon
pinch of fine sea salt

Citrus syrup:
scant 2/3 cup (125g) superfine
    sugar
1/2 cup (125ml) water
finely pared zest and juice of
    1 lemon
finely pared zest and juice of
    1 orange
1 tsp (5ml) orange-flower water
(or rose water)

Preheat the oven to 350°F (180°C). Butter the base and sides of a 9–10-inch (23–25cm) round cake pan with removable base and line the base with a disk of baking parchment.

Beat the egg yolks and sugar together with a handheld electric whisk until pale and creamy. Sift the flour over the surface and fold in gently. Add the yogurt, lemon zest, and juice, and fold through.

In another large, clean bowl, whisk the egg whites with a pinch of salt until firm peaks form. Carefully fold them into the cake batter, using a large metal spoon.

Pour the batter into the prepared cake pan and gently level the surface. Bake in the oven for 50 to 60 minutes until the cake is golden brown on top, risen, and cooked through. To test, insert a skewer into the middle; it should come out clean. Let cool completely in the pan; the cake will sink slightly as it cools.

While the cake is in the oven, prepare the citrus syrup. Put all of the ingredients into a saucepan and bring to a boil. Lower the heat slightly and simmer for about 7 to 10 minutes until it has reduced by a third and is syrupy. Let cool, then pour into a serving pitcher.

Turn the cake out onto a large plate or cake stand and spoon some citrus syrup evenly all over the surface. Serve with some crème fraîche or thick yogurt on the side, if you like.

Almond
semolina cake

THIS DELICIOUS LEBANESE CAKE is known as *sfouf* and acquires its lovely yellow color from the inclusion of a little turmeric. This is a fairly large cake, but one that keeps well in an airtight container in the refrigerator for up to 5 days. Serve with hot mint tea or Turkish coffee at the end of a meal, or at coffee time.

SERVES 10–12

butter, for greasing
2¹/₂ cups (450g) fine semolina
generous 1 cup (150g) all-purpose flour
2 tsp (10ml) baking powder
1 tsp (5ml) ground turmeric
2¹/₄ cups (450g) superfine sugar
generous 2 cups (550ml) whole milk
2 large eggs, lightly beaten
generous ³/₄ cup (200g) lightly salted butter, melted
1 tsp (5ml) orange-flower water (or rose water)
scant ¹/₄ cup (25g) slivered almonds
2 tbsp (10ml) apricot jam, warmed, to glaze
    (optional)

To serve (optional):
thick yogurt
runny honey, to drizzle

Preheat the oven to 350°F (180°C). Lightly butter a 9-inch (23cm) square cake pan (or a 9¹/₂-inch/24cm round pan), preferably with a removable base, and line the base with baking parchment.

In a large bowl, combine the semolina, flour, baking powder, and turmeric. Stir to mix, then make a well in the center.

In a separate bowl, mix the sugar, milk, eggs, melted butter, and orange-flower water together until evenly blended. Pour into the well in the dry ingredients and fold together until well combined. Pour the batter into the prepared cake pan and sprinkle the almonds over the surface.

Bake for 40 to 50 minutes until the top is golden brown and the cake is cooked through. To test, insert a skewer into the center; it should come out clean. Leave in the pan for about 15 to 20 minutes before unmolding onto a wire rack to cool. If you wish, brush the top of the cake with a little apricot jam to glaze.

Slice the cake and serve—either on its own or with a dollop of yogurt drizzled with a little honey.

CHINESE

A MEAL AT OUR FAVORITE LOCAL CHINESE IS ALWAYS
A TREAT—THE KIDS LOVE IT AND I ENCOURAGE THEM
TO TRY SOMETHING DIFFERENT EACH TIME. NOT
SURPRISINGLY, AS CHINA IS SUCH A VAST COUNTRY,
THE COOKING VARIES SIGNIFICANTLY FROM ONE REGION
TO ANOTHER. GINGER, GARLIC, AND GREEN ONIONS
ARE COMMON INGREDIENTS. TOGETHER WITH VARIOUS
SOY SAUCES, THEY ARE USED TO CREATE ALL MANNER
OF TASTY DISHES. IF YOU ONLY COOK ONE RECIPE FROM
THIS CHAPTER, MAKE IT THE PORK FLANK—IT MELTS
IN THE MOUTH AND THE FLAVOR IS SUBLIME.

Corn and crab soup

ORIGINALLY CREATED BY CHINESE EMIGRANTS in America, this easy soup now appears on Chinese restaurant menus in most countries. Creamed corn provides the right texture for the soup, but if you are having difficulty finding it, buy canned corn kernels and pulse them in a food processor to a rough purée.

SERVES 4–6

4oz (125g) white crabmeat

2 large egg whites

1 tbsp (15ml) cornstarch, mixed with 2 tbsp (30ml) water

5 cups (1.2 liters) chicken stock

1-inch (2.5cm) piece of gingerroot, peeled and grated

8oz (225g) can creamed corn

sea salt and white pepper

2 green onions, trimmed and finely sliced

Pick through the crabmeat with your fingers and remove any stray fragments of shell. In another bowl, lightly beat the egg whites until frothy. Add them to the crabmeat along with the blended cornstarch and stir well.

Pour the stock into a saucepan, add the gingerroot and bring to a simmer. Tip in the corn and bring back to a boil. Lower the heat slightly and simmer for a few minutes. Stir in the crabmeat mixture and some seasoning. Simmer gently, stirring, for a few minutes until the soup has thickened. Taste and adjust the seasoning.

Ladle the soup into warm bowls and scatter the green onion slices on top. Serve immediately.

Crispy salt and pepper squid
with cucumber salad

DEEP-FRIED SQUID IS A MUCH-LOVED DISH and almost every cuisine seems to have a different version. Here Szechuan pepper and five-spice powder give the squid an extra kick. When deep-frying, keep the oil at a constant high temperature to ensure the squid cooks and crispens quickly. Avoid overcooking, otherwise the squid will turn tough and rubbery.

SERVES 4

14oz (400g) baby squid, cleaned
1/2 tsp (2ml) Szechuan
    peppercorns
1 tsp (5ml) sea salt
1 tsp (5ml) freshly ground
    black pepper
1/4 tsp (1ml) five-spice powder
5 heaping tbsp (75ml) cornstarch
vegetable or peanut oil, for
    deep-frying

Cucumber salad:
1 medium cucumber
1 medium carrot
1 red chile, seeded and finely
    sliced
handful of cilantro leaves
3 tbsp (45ml) rice vinegar
1/2 tsp (2ml) sea salt
1 tsp (5ml) superfine sugar
1 tsp (5ml) sesame oil

To serve:
1 red chile, trimmed and finely
    sliced, to garnish
small handful of cilantro leaves,
    to garnish
lime wedges

First, prepare the cucumber salad. Peel the cucumber and carrot, then slice into long strips, using a vegetable peeler or a mandolin. Cut the strips in half if they are too long. Toss them in a bowl with the red chile and cilantro leaves. In a small bowl, mix together the rice vinegar, salt, sugar, and sesame oil; set aside.

Slice the squid pouches into thick rings, leaving the tentacles whole. Rinse and pat dry with paper towels. Using a mortar and pestle, grind the Szechuan peppercorns with the salt to a fine powder. Tip into a small bowl and mix in the black pepper, five-spice powder, and cornstarch.

Heat a 2-inch (5cm) depth of oil in a wok over high heat until a piece of bread dropped into the hot oil sizzles vigorously. Deep-fry the squid rings and tentacles in batches: coat with the seasoned cornstarch, shake off excess, then immerse in the hot oil, taking care not to overcrowd the wok. Deep-fry for about a minute until lightly golden and crisp, then remove with a slotted spoon and drain on paper towels. Keep warm in a low oven while you deep-fry the rest of the squid.

Toss the cucumber salad with the dressing and divide between serving plates. Pile the crispy squid on top and scatter over the sliced chile and cilantro leaves. Serve with lime wedges.

Shaping Chinese dumplings

On a lightly floured counter, roll out the pie dough into a long sausage, about 1 inch (2.5cm) thick. Cut into 3/4-inch (2cm) lengths. Flatten each piece with the palm of your hand, then roll out into a thin circle, approximately 3 1/2 inches (9cm) in diameter.

Put 1–1 1/2 teaspoons (5–7.5ml) of filling in the center of a circle and brush the rim of the dough with a little water. Fold the sides up over the filling to meet, creating a half-moon shape. Now carefully pinch the edges of the dough together using your fingertips, making small folds, or pleats, along one side. Set aside. Repeat to make the rest of the dumplings.

Pork and shrimp dumplings

MAKING CHINESE DUMPLINGS is a labor of love, requiring patience, time, and practice. If you are going to the effort, it is worth making a large batch so that you can freeze some for another meal. Freeze, uncooked, on a tray lined with parchment, then pack into a rigid container. Defrost at room temperature before cooking.

MAKES 30–35

Pie dough:

2¼ cups (300g) all-purpose flour, plus extra to dust
1 tsp (5ml) fine sea salt
1 tbsp (15ml) vegetable oil
½–⅔ cup (120–150ml) cold water

Filling:

7oz (200g) Chinese cabbage leaves
sea salt and white pepper
9oz (250g) ground pork
7oz (200g) raw shrimp, peeled, deveined, and minced
1¼-inch (3cm) piece of gingerroot, peeled and grated
1 tsp (5ml) soft light brown sugar
2 tbsp (30ml) light soy sauce
1 tbsp (15ml) Chinese rice wine (or dry sherry)
2 tsp (10ml) sesame oil

Dipping sauce:

2 tbsp (30ml) red chili oil (available from Asian grocers)
1 tbsp (15ml) light soy sauce
1 large garlic clove, peeled and minced
1 green onion, trimmed, green part only, finely sliced

To make the dough for the dumplings, mix the flour and salt together in a large bowl and make a well in the center. Add the oil and ½ cup (120ml) water. Mix with a round-bladed knife until the mixture starts to come together as a firm dough. Add a little more water if it seems too dry. Knead the dough on a lightly floured counter for 5 to 10 minutes until silky. Shape into a ball, wrap in plastic wrap, and let rest while you make the filling.

For the filling, add the cabbage leaves to a pan of boiling salted water and blanch for 2 to 3 minutes until just wilted. Drain well and pat dry with paper towels. Mince the leaves and place in a large bowl. Add the rest of the filling ingredients and mix well. To check the seasoning, cook off a little ball of the mixture in an oiled pan, then taste for seasoning. Adjust the seasoning of the uncooked filling mixture as necessary.

Now roll out the dough and shape the dumplings, following my guide (on the preceding pages).

You will need to cook the dumplings in batches. Steam them in a bamboo steamer lined with baking parchment for 7 to 10 minutes until just cooked through (or you can poach them in a light stock for 5 minutes if you prefer, then drain well).

While the dumplings are cooking, mix all the ingredients for the dipping sauce together and divide between individual dipping bowls. Serve the dumplings, freshly cooked and piping hot, with the dipping sauce.

Steamed bream with ginger and green onions

STEAMING WHOLE FISH IN THIS WAY enables you to retain all of its wonderful, flavorful juices and gives you a lovely, aromatic sauce—perfect for spooning over accompanying plain white rice.

SERVES 4

1 bream, scaled and cleaned, about 1¹/₂lb (700g)
1¹/₂-inch (4cm) piece of gingerroot, peeled
4 green onions, trimmed
1 long red chile, seeded
2 tbsp (30ml) Shaoxing or Chinese rice wine (or dry sherry)
2 tbsp (30ml) light soy sauce
2 tbsp (30ml) sesame oil

Make slashes in the fish, about 1 inch (2.5cm) apart, slightly on the diagonal, without cutting right through to the bone. Slice the gingerroot, green onions, and red chile lengthwise into thin sticks.

Scatter a little ginger and green onion over a heatproof plate, large enough to take the fish. Lay the bream on the plate and stuff the fish cavity with a little gingerroot, green onion, and chile. Drizzle the rice wine and soy sauce over the fish, then scatter over the rest of the gingerroot, green onion, and chile.

Place an inverted heatproof bowl in a large wok and pour in enough water to come halfway up the sides of the bowl. Put the lid on the wok and bring the water to a boil. Now carefully lower the plate containing the fish into the pan, placing it on the upturned bowl; avoid touching the sides of the hot wok. Put the lid back on and steam over high heat until the fish is just cooked—a knife should slide easily into the thickest part of the flesh. It will take about 10 to 15 minutes.

As soon as the fish is ready, carefully lift the plate from the steamer. Heat the sesame oil in a small pan until smoking hot, then immediately pour over the fish. Bring the plate to the table and serve at once, with rice and a vegetable dish on the side.

Red braised pork flank

REPUTED TO BE MAO ZEDONG'S FAVORITE dish, this
is a specialty of Hunan, his home region. It is irresistibly rich and truly
delicious. Enjoy with a simple bowl of steamed white rice and pak choi
or a mixed vegetable stir-fry.

SERVES 4–6

1³/₄lb (800g) pork flank
1 tbsp (15ml) vegetable oil
2 tbsp (30ml) rock sugar
   (or superfine sugar)
3 tbsp (45ml) light soy sauce
3 tbsp (45ml) dark soy sauce
1¹/₄-inch (3cm) piece of
   gingerroot, peeled and thickly
   sliced
2 star anise
1 cinnamon stick
3 dried red chiles
about ³/₄ cup (200ml) water
3 green onions, trimmed and
   chopped

Bring a wide pan of water to a boil, then reduce the heat slightly. Lower
the pork flank into the pan (cut in half if it doesn't fit in whole) and
simmer for 3 to 4 minutes. Skim off the scum and froth from the surface;
there will be a lot of it. Drain the pork flank and let cool slightly. Rinse
out the pan and return to the stove.

Cut the pork flank into ³/₄-inch (2cm) cubes. Heat the oil and sugar in
the pan over medium heat. Once the sugar is melted and beginning to
caramelize, add the pork pieces, skin-side down, and pan-fry for a few
minutes until the skin begins to caramelize.

Add the soy sauces, gingerroot, star anise, cinnamon, and dried chiles
to the pan and pour in enough water to just cover the meat. Bring to
a gentle simmer and cook for about 50 to 60 minutes until the pork is
very tender.

Remove the pork with a slotted spoon and set aside on a plate. Boil the
sauce until reduced and syrupy, then taste and adjust the seasoning,
adding a little more sugar if you find it too salty. Stir in the green onions,
reserving a handful for serving, and return the pork pieces to the pan to
warm through.

Pile the pork into a warm bowl, sprinkle with the remaining green onions
and serve at once.

Five-spice roast duck with plum sauce

THIS TENDER AROMATIC DUCK is perfectly complemented by my spiced fresh plum sauce. Serve it topped with shredded green onions and cucumber, and if you wish, accompany with thin, ready-made Chinese pancakes. Any leftovers will be lovely with noodles.

SERVES 6–8

1 duckling, about 5lb (2.25kg)
1 tsp (5ml) sea salt
1 tsp (5ml) five-spice powder
1 tsp (5ml) black pepper
1 tbsp (15ml) soy sauce
2 tbsp (30ml) runny honey
2 tbsp (30ml) Chinese black vinegar (or lemon juice)

Fresh plum sauce:
1 tbsp (15ml) vegetable oil
1 tsp (5ml) grated gingerroot
3 ripe plums, pitted and chopped
1/2 tsp (2ml) five-spice powder
1 small cinnamon stick
2 star anise
2 tbsp (30ml) Chinese rice vinegar
4 tbsp (60ml) soft brown sugar
1–2 tbsp (15–30ml) water

To serve:
thinly shredded green onions
thinly sliced cucumber

Preheat the oven to 425°F (220°C). Remove as much fat as possible from around the neck of the duck. In a small bowl, mix together the salt, five-spice powder, and pepper. Lightly score the skin of the duck, then rub the seasoning mixture all over the skin and into the cuts.

Place the duck, breast-side up, on a wire rack set on top of a roasting tray. Place in the hot oven and roast for 30 minutes.

In the meantime, mix the soy sauce, honey, and Chinese vinegar together in a small bowl. Carefully baste the duck with the soy mixture and pour a cupful of water into the roasting tray. Lower the oven setting to 375°F (190°C) and roast the duck for another 1 1/4 to 1 1/2 hours, basting every half-hour or so, until it is tender and just cooked through.

While the duck is roasting, make the plum sauce. Heat a little oil in a pan, add the ginger, and cook until lightly golden, about 1 to 2 minutes. Tip in the chopped plums, five-spice powder, cinnamon, star anise, rice vinegar, and sugar. Stir well and simmer for about 15 minutes until the mixture has a thick, jammy consistency. Transfer to a serving bowl. The sauce can be served warm or at room temperature.

Once the duck is cooked, cover loosely with foil and let rest in a warm place for 15 to 20 minutes. Carve and arrange on a large platter. Scatter over some shredded green onions and sliced cucumber and serve, with the plum sauce.

5 ways with Chinese greens

Chinese **broccoli** with **oyster sauce**

Trim 1lb (450g) Chinese broccoli (kai lan), wash, and drain well, then cut into finger lengths. In a bowl, mix 1 tbsp (15ml) Chinese rice wine (or dry sherry), 1/4 tsp (1ml) superfine sugar, 3 tbsp (45ml) oyster sauce, and 1/2 tsp (2ml) sesame oil with 4 tbsp (60ml) vegetable or chicken stock. In a large wok or skillet, heat 1 tbsp (15ml) peanut oil over medium heat. Add 3 lightly smashed garlic cloves and cook until lightly golden, then add a grated 11/4-inch (3cm) piece of gingerroot and sauté for 30 seconds. Tip in the Chinese broccoli and stir-fry for 30 seconds. Pour in the sauce, put the lid on, and let the vegetables steam for 2 to 3 minutes until the broccoli is tender. Serve immediately, with steamed rice. **SERVES 4**

Chinese **cabbage stir-fried** with **gingerroot**

Heat 1 tbsp (15ml) peanut oil in a wok. Add a grated 11/4-inch (3cm) piece of gingerroot and sauté over high heat for less than a minute until fragrant. Stir in 7oz (200g) baby corn, halved lengthwise, and 71/2oz (220g) halved, canned water chestnuts and sauté for another minute. Add a thinly sliced 1/2 head of Chinese cabbage, 4 sliced green onions, 1 tbsp (15ml) light soy sauce, 2 tbsp (30ml) oyster sauce, and 2 tsp (10ml) sesame oil. Stir-fry for 2 to 3 minutes until the cabbage and corn are just tender. **SERVES 4**

Braised **pak choi**

Heat 1 tbsp (15ml) each peanut and sesame oils in a large sauté pan or wok over medium heat. Add a grated 1-inch (2.5cm) piece of gingerroot and 2 minced garlic cloves and sauté, stirring, for about a minute until fragrant. Halve 1lb (450g) pak choi lengthwise and place in the pan, cut-side down. Sauté for a minute or so, turning occasionally. Mix together 4 tbsp (60ml) chicken or vegetable stock, 1 tbsp (15ml) light soy sauce, 1 tbsp (15ml) dark soy sauce, and 1 tbsp (15ml) brown sugar and pour over the pak choi. Simmer for 3 to 5 minutes until the pak choi is tender, but retaining a slight crunch. Serve immediately. **SERVES 4**

Spicy Chinese **greens**

Cut 14oz (400g) choi sum or pak choi leaves into thirds. Add to a pan of boiling water and blanch for 2 to 3 minutes until the leaves have just wilted, the stalks retaining a crunch. Drain, refresh in ice water, and drain well. Heat 2 tbsp (30ml) peanut oil in a wok or sauté pan over medium-high heat. Add 3 minced garlic cloves and 2 finely sliced red chiles and sauté for 30 seconds until fragrant. Add the blanched greens and toss well. Add 2 tbsp (30ml) soy sauce, 1 tbsp (15ml) oyster sauce, and a grinding of white pepper. Stir-fry until piping hot. **SERVES 4**

Stir-fried Chinese **spinach**

Place a wok over high heat and add 4 tsp (20ml) peanut oil. When hot, add 3 minced garlic cloves and toss for 30 seconds until lightly golden. Add 1lb (500g) Chinese spinach and stir-fry for 1 to 2 minutes until the leaves are just wilted. Add 2 tsp (10ml) spicy fermented bean paste, 4 tsp (20ml) oyster sauce, and a good grinding of white pepper. Stir-fry until the greens are nicely coated in the sauce. Serve immediately. **SERVES 4**

Green beans and mushrooms in black bean sauce

THIS IS A QUICK, TASTY STIR-FRY of vegetables. Fermented black soybeans—sometimes labeled as salted black beans—are available from Asian grocers and selected supermarkets. They are, in fact, salted, fermented, and dried beans, which may also be flavored with chile or gingerroot. They are normally rinsed before cooking to remove some of the excess salt.

SERVES 4

14oz (400g) green beans, trimmed
8oz (225g) shiitake mushrooms, cleaned
2 tbsp (30ml) vegetable or peanut oil
1 tbsp (15ml) fermented black beans, rinsed and
   dried
2 large garlic cloves, peeled and chopped

Sauce:
2 tbsp (30ml) Chinese rice vinegar
2 tbsp (30ml) Shaoxing or Chinese rice wine
   (or dry sherry)
2 tbsp (30ml) light soy sauce
1 tbsp (15ml) oyster sauce
1 tsp (5ml) superfine sugar
1 tsp (5ml) cornstarch, mixed with 2 tbsp
   (30ml) water

Cut the green beans into finger lengths and finely slice the mushrooms. Mix together all the ingredients for the sauce in a bowl and set aside.

Heat the oil in a wok over medium-high heat. Tip in the black beans and garlic and sauté for 30 seconds or so, until fragrant. Add the green beans with a little splash of water. Stir-fry for 2 minutes, then add the mushrooms. Stir-fry for another minute or two.

Pour the sauce over the vegetables and toss well. Simmer for a couple of minutes until the sauce begins to thicken and the green beans are tender but still retain a slight crunch. Transfer to a warm plate and bring to the table.

Cantonese fried rice

THIS IS A GREAT WAY TO USE UP LEFTOVER RICE—in fact it works better, as it is less sticky and easier to cook than freshly steamed rice. (Note, however, that leftover rice should be refrigerated and used within a day of cooking.) You can replace the shrimp with diced chicken, roast pork, or ham, and vary the vegetables—diced peppers, zucchini, and corn all work well.

SERVES 4

4oz (120g) raw shrimp, peeled
4 tbsp (60ml) vegetable or peanut oil
1 onion, peeled and chopped
2 large garlic cloves, peeled and minced
1 carrot, peeled and diced
sea salt and white pepper
scant 1/2 cup (50g) peas, thawed if frozen
2 medium eggs, beaten with a pinch of salt
about 2 1/4 cups (400g) day-old cooked rice
3–4 green onions, trimmed and chopped
2 tbsp (30ml) light soy sauce, or to taste

Devein the shrimp and if they are quite large, roughly chop them; cover and set aside.

Heat half the oil in a wok over medium-high heat. Add the onion, garlic, carrot, and a pinch each of salt and pepper. Stir-fry for about 2 to 3 minutes until the vegetables begin to soften.

Tip in the shrimp and peas and stir-fry until the shrimp begin to turn pink. Push the ingredients to one side of the wok and add a little more oil to the other. Add the beaten eggs to the oil and cook, stirring occasionally, to scramble them. Once they are almost set, stir them through the rest of the ingredients.

If necessary, add a little more oil to the wok and then tip in the rice and green onions. Season with some soy sauce and stir-fry for 3 to 4 minutes until the rice is piping hot. Taste and adjust the seasoning before serving.

Fruit salad
with star anise syrup

A SIMPLE PLATTER OF FRESH FRUIT, such as sliced oranges, typically finishes a Chinese meal. Following the same principle, this exotic fruit salad is a light and refreshing finale. There are no hard and fast rules—treat the selection below merely as a suggestion and adapt it to include any fruit in season.

SERVES 4

7oz (200g) lychees
1 large ripe mango
1 carambola, trimmed
1 large dragon fruit
2 persimmons

Star anise syrup:
generous $1/3$ cup (75g) superfine
  sugar
juice of 1 lime
2 star anise
$2/3$ cup (150ml) water

To serve (optional):
few mint leaves, shredded
small handful of cilantro leaves

First, make the star anise syrup. Put the sugar, lime juice, star anise, and water into a saucepan and stir over medium heat until the sugar dissolves. Increase the heat slightly and boil for 7 to 8 minutes until thickened to a light syrup. Take off the heat and let cool completely.

Prepare the fruit: peel and pit the lychees; peel, seed, and slice the mango; slice the carambola; cut the dragon fruit into wedges; peel the persimmons and cut into wedges.

Arrange the fruits attractively on a large platter and drizzle the star anise syrup over them (you may not need all of it; keep any extra in the refrigerator to drizzle over other fruit salads). Cover the platter with plastic wrap and chill for 30 minutes before serving.

Scatter over the shredded mint and cilantro leaves to serve, if using.

Wonton and sesame twists with sesame ice cream

THIS ICE CREAM MAY NOT LOOK INVITING, but it has a wonderfully intense sesame flavor. For a milder taste—and more enticing color— use white, rather than black sesame seeds. The crispy wonton and sesame twists add an interesting texture, but if you haven't time to make them, serve dessert cookies instead.

SERVES 4

Sesame ice cream:
1/2 cup (85g) black (or white) sesame seeds
4 large egg yolks
1/2 cup (100g) superfine sugar
generous 1 cup (250ml) whole milk
generous 1 cup (250ml) heavy cream

Wonton and sesame twists:
8 wonton wrappers, thawed if frozen
1 medium egg, lightly beaten
1 tbsp (15ml) black (or white) sesame seeds (or a combination)
vegetable or peanut oil, for cooking
confectioners' sugar, to dust

To make the ice cream, toast the sesame seeds in a dry pan, tossing frequently, until fragrant and lightly golden. Tip onto a plate and let cool, then finely grind in a small food processor to a fine paste.

Beat the egg yolks and sugar together in a bowl until creamy. Put the milk and half of the cream into a heavy saucepan over medium heat. Simmer gently for a minute, then whisk a little of the warm, creamy milk into the sugary yolks. Now gradually whisk this into the milk in the pan. Stir with a wooden spoon over medium-low heat until the custard is thickened enough to lightly coat the back of the spoon.

Add the sesame paste to the hot custard. (For a smooth texture, press through a strainer.) Set over a bowl of ice water to cool quickly. In another bowl, whip the remaining cream to soft peaks, then fold through the cooled custard. Pour into an ice-cream machine and churn until almost frozen. Transfer to a suitable container and freeze until firm.

To make the wonton and sesame twists, cut each wonton wrapper into 4 long strips. Make a lengthwise slit in the center of each (like a button-hole) and push one end through to create a twist. Brush the twists with beaten egg and then lightly coat with sesame seeds. Lay on a board.

Heat a 1 1/4–1 1/2-inch (3–4cm) depth of oil in a wok or heavy deep pan until hot. Cook the twists in batches until crisp and golden all over, about 1 to 2 minutes on each side. Remove with a slotted spoon and drain on paper towels. Cool, then dust with confectioners' sugar before serving.

To serve, place one or two scoops of sesame ice cream in each bowl and add a few sesame and wonton twists.

THAI

ABOVE ALL ELSE, THAI FOOD IS WONDERFULLY
FRAGRANT. THE USE OF INGREDIENTS, SUCH AS
LIMES, COCONUT, LEMONGRASS, AND LIME LEAVES,
MAKE THE FOOD ENTICINGLY AROMATIC. IT CAN
SOMETIMES BE VERY FIERY, TOO, BUT ALWAYS FULL
OF FANTASTIC FLAVORS. I SEE IT AS A VERY HEALTHY
FOOD AND IT HAS A REAL FEEL GOOD FACTOR WHEN
YOU EAT IT. AS WITH INDIAN FOOD THERE IS SO MUCH
MORE TO THAI COOKING THAN CURRIES. ONE WORD
OF ADVICE: NEVER SKIMP ON THE QUALITY OF THE
INGREDIENTS. THE KEY TO THAI FOOD IS FRESHNESS,
SO EVERYTHING MUST BE IN PEAK CONDITION.

Fishcakes with spicy cucumber relish

CURRIED SHRIMP AND WHITE FISHCAKES are a real treat, but you do need to enjoy them freshly cooked, as they do not reheat well. Also, to ensure the patties have an interesting texture, it is important to avoid overblending the fish and shrimp mixture.

MAKES 10–12

9oz (250g) skinless white fish
  fillets
9oz (250g) large shrimp, peeled
  and deveined
1 tbsp Thai red curry paste
1 kaffir lime leaf, finely shredded
  (or finely grated zest of 1 lime)
1 tbsp (15ml) chopped cilantro
1 medium egg
1 tsp (5ml) brown sugar
1 tsp (5ml) fish sauce
pinch of sea salt
1/4 cup (30g) fine green beans,
  trimmed and thinly sliced
vegetable oil, for shallow-frying

Spicy cucumber relish:
1 cucumber
1/2 small red chile, seeded and
  thinly sliced
1 shallot, peeled and finely sliced
juice of 2 limes
2 tbsp (30ml) superfine sugar
1/2 tsp (2ml) sea salt
2–3 tbsp (30–45ml) water
small handful of cilantro, leaves
  roughly chopped
small handful of mint, leaves
  roughly chopped

First, make the spicy cucumber relish. Peel the cucumber and quarter lengthwise, then scoop out the seeds in the center with a teaspoon. Thinly slice the cucumber on the diagonal and place in a large bowl. Add the chile and shallot, toss to mix, and set aside.

Put the lime juice, sugar, salt, and water into a small saucepan and bring to a simmer, stirring well to dissolve the sugar. Let simmer for a few minutes until slightly thickened, then set aside to cool completely.

Put all the ingredients for the fishcakes, except the green beans and oil, into a food processor and pulse to a finely chopped wet paste. Do not overprocess, as you want to keep some texture to the fishcakes.

Scrape the mixture into a bowl and stir in the green beans. To check the seasoning, cook off a little ball of mixture in an oiled pan and taste, then adjust the seasoning of the uncooked mixture accordingly, adding a little more salt and/or sugar as necessary. With wet hands, shape the mixture into small patties about 2 inches (5cm) in diameter, each from about 2 tablespoonfuls (30ml) of mixture.

Heat a 3/4–11/4-inch (2–3cm) depth of oil in a deep skillet or wok. Shallow-fry the patties in batches for 1 to 2 minutes on each side, until golden brown. Drain on a tray lined with paper towels and keep warm in a low oven while you cook the rest.

When the fishcakes are all cooked, pour the dressing over the cucumber relish and stir in the chopped herbs. Serve the fishcakes hot, with the cucumber relish on the side.

Chicken in spicy coconut broth

THIS WONDERFULLY AROMATIC SOUP, called *tom ka gai*, is one of my favorite Thai appetizers. It is incredibly easy to make and cooks in next to no time. For a quick midweek supper, serve larger bowls—tossing in some blanched rice noodles and a handful of beansprouts and cilantro leaves. Simple and delicious.

SERVES 4–6

2 boneless, skinless chicken breasts, about 9oz (250g)
sea salt and black pepper
14oz (400ml) can reduced-fat coconut milk
2½ cups (600ml) water
1¼-inch (3cm) piece of gingerroot, peeled and sliced
4 kaffir lime leaves, torn in half (or pared zest of 1 lime)
1 lemongrass stalk, trimmed and halved lengthwise
2 red chiles, halved lengthwise and seeded
1 tbsp (15ml) palm sugar (or soft light brown sugar)
2½ tbsp (37.5ml) fish sauce
2 tbsp (30ml) lime juice, or to taste
3½oz (100g) white mushrooms, cleaned
handful of cilantro leaves, to garnish

Thinly slice the chicken breasts, cutting across the grain, into bite-size pieces. Place in a bowl, season with a little salt and pepper, and set aside.

Pour the coconut milk into a saucepan, then add the 2½ cups (600ml) water, using the can as a measure (i.e. 1½ cans). Add the gingerroot, kaffir lime leaves, lemongrass, chiles, sugar, fish sauce, and lime juice. Bring to a simmer and cook gently, stirring occasionally, for about 5 minutes to allow the flavors to infuse.

Add the mushrooms to the broth and simmer for 2 to 3 minutes. Add the chicken, stir, and simmer until cooked through; this will only take 1 to 2 minutes. Taste and adjust the seasoning if you need to.

Serve the soup in warm bowls, discarding the gingerroot, lemongrass, chiles, and lime leaves if you wish; traditionally, these aromatics are left in the soup but not eaten. Garnish each bowl with some cilantro leaves and serve immediately.

Thai red curry paste

You will need 6–7 long, red chiles. To prepare, roll each chile between your fingers to loosen the seeds, then cut off the stem end and squeeze out the seeds. Chop the chiles, then wash your hands thoroughly.

To make the red curry paste, put the chiles into a food processor with 4 chopped shallots, 5–6 chopped garlic cloves, a 1½-inch (4cm) chopped piece of gingerroot, 1 trimmed and minced lemongrass stalk, 1 minced kaffir lime leaf (or the grated zest of 1 lime), and a handful of chopped cilantro stems. Grind to a fine paste, adding 1–2 tbsp (15–30ml) vegetable oil as necessary.

Grind 1 tsp (5ml) each lightly toasted coriander and cumin seeds with 1½ tsp (7.5ml) black peppercorns and 1 tsp (5ml) sea salt to a fine powder, using a mortar and pestle. Tip this into the food processor and add 1 tsp (5ml) shrimp paste, if you like. Blend until finely ground and well combined; you will need to stop the machine to scrape down the side of the bowl a few times to get an evenly ground wet paste. Store the curry paste in a screw-topped jar, refrigerate, and use within a week. **MAKES ABOUT 10OZ (280g)**

Pork satay with peanut sauce

SATAY IS A POPULAR STREET FOOD in Thailand. I've used pork here, but it is also made with chicken, beef, squid, and shrimp. For optimum flavor, allow the pork plenty of time to marinate; this also helps to tenderize the meat. Satay is best cooked on the barbecue as it takes on a slightly smoky flavor, but you can, of course, use the broiler or a griddle pan.

SERVES 4-6

1 lb (500g) pork loin or tenderloin
1/2 cup (125ml) canned coconut milk
1 1/4-inch (3cm) piece of gingerroot, peeled and grated
1 lemongrass stalk, trimmed and white part minced
1 tsp (5ml) ground turmeric
2 tsp (10ml) ground coriander
2 tsp (10ml) ground cumin
1/2 tsp (2ml) sea salt
freshly ground black pepper
1-2 tsp (5-10ml) superfine sugar
vegetable or peanut oil, for brushing

Thai peanut sauce:
2/3 cup (100g) roasted skinned peanuts (unsalted)
generous 3/4 cup (200ml) canned coconut milk
4-5 tbsp (60-75ml) Thai red curry paste (to make your own, see page 186)
1 1/2 tsp (7.5ml) sea salt
1-2 tbsp (15-30ml) palm sugar (or soft light brown sugar)
2-3 tbsp (30-45ml) tamarind paste (or lime juice)

Slice the pork into long, thin strips across the grain. Mix the rest of the ingredients, except the oil, together in a large bowl, add the pork, and toss to coat well. Cover with plastic wrap and let marinate in the refrigerator for at least an hour, preferably overnight, to allow the flavors to develop. Soak 8-12 bamboo skewers in warm water (this will prevent them from scorching under the broiler).

Meanwhile, make the peanut sauce. Pulse the peanuts in a food processor until minced very finely (or coarsely ground), then tip into a bowl. Spoon the thick creamy layer of the coconut milk into a saucepan. Heat gently and when the oil separates from the milk, add the curry paste and cook until it is fragrant.

Now add the remaining coconut milk and the minced peanuts. Stir in the salt, sugar, and tamarind paste and simmer gently, stirring frequently, until the sauce thickens. (If the sauce is too thick, stir in a little boiling water.) Pour into a bowl and allow to cool completely.

Heat up the barbecue, broiler, or griddle pan. Thread the marinated pork slices onto the presoaked bamboo skewers. Brush with a little oil to prevent them from sticking and drying out and cook for 1 1/2 to 2 minutes on each side. Serve hot, with the peanut sauce for dipping.

Red snapper with chili, tamarind, and lime sauce

THIS IS MY TAKE ON A DISH I ENJOYED in Thailand several years ago—a whole crispy pan-fried pomfret smothered in a delicious sweet, sour, and hot tamarind sauce. Utterly divine. My healthier version uses red snapper fillets, but you can use any firm white fish for this recipe.

SERVES 4

4 red snapper fillets, about
    4oz (120g) each
sea salt and black pepper
2 tbsp (30ml) vegetable or
    peanut oil
handful of baby spinach leaves
    (optional)

Sauce:
4 tsp (20ml) vegetable or
    peanut oil
4 long red chiles, seeded and
    chopped
6 garlic cloves, peeled and
    chopped
4 green onions, trimmed and
    finely sliced on the diagonal
2 tbsp (30ml) lime juice
4 tbsp (60ml) tamarind paste (or
    lime juice)
2 tbsp (30ml) soy sauce
2 tbsp (30ml) fish sauce
2 tsp (10ml) palm sugar (or soft
    light brown sugar)
2 tbsp (30ml) water

Check the fish fillets for small bones, removing any you find with kitchen tweezers. Set aside at room temperature while you prepare the sauce.

For the sauce, heat the oil in a saucepan over medium heat. Add the chiles and garlic and cook, stirring frequently, for 1 to 2 minutes until fragrant. Add the rest of the ingredients, stir well, and simmer gently for about 5 to 10 minutes until the sauce has reduced to a light jammy consistency. If it thickens too much, add a touch more water to thin it down slightly.

Season the red snapper fillets with salt and pepper. Heat the oil in a wide (preferably nonstick) skillet. Pan-fry the fish fillets, skin-side down, for $1^{1}/_{2}$ minutes until the skin is lightly golden brown and the fish is cooked two-thirds of the way up. Flip the fish fillets over and cook the other side for about 30 seconds just until the flesh turns opaque and feels just firm.

To serve, spoon the sauce onto warm plates. If you wish, scatter over a layer of spinach leaves before arranging a fish fillet on each plate. Serve immediately, with plain jasmine rice.

Fragrant green curry with beef

YOU CAN USE ANY TENDER MEAT OR POULTRY, or firm-fleshed fish you fancy for this curry. The "green" in the curry paste tends to become muted upon cooking, but the fragrance and flavors will intensify with heat. Use fewer chiles if you prefer a milder curry. You will have more green curry paste than you need for this recipe, but like the red curry paste (on page 186), it can be stored in a screw-topped jar in the refrigerator for up to a week.

SERVES 4

Green curry paste:
10 long, green chiles
3 shallots, peeled
6 garlic cloves, peeled
1½-inch (4cm) piece of gingerroot, peeled
bunch of cilantro, stems only
2 lemongrass stalks, trimmed
3 kaffir lime leaves (or finely grated zest of 2 limes)
1–2 tbsp (15–30ml) vegetable oil
1 tbsp (15ml) coriander seeds
1 tsp (5ml) cumin seeds
½ tsp (2ml) black peppercorns
1 tsp (5ml) sea salt
1 tsp (5ml) shrimp paste (optional)

Beef curry:
1lb (450g) beef tenderloin
5 baby eggplants, (or 1 small regular one), trimmed
1 tbsp (15ml) vegetable oil
14oz (400ml) can coconut milk
2 red chiles, halved lengthwise
2 kaffir lime leaves, torn in half
4 tsp (20ml) fish sauce
1 tsp (5ml) brown sugar
handful of shredded Thai sweet basil or cilantro

First, make the curry paste. Roughly chop the green chiles, shallots, garlic, gingerroot, and cilantro stems and place in a food processor. Mince the lemongrass and lime leaves, add these to the processor, and grind to a fine paste, adding 1–2 tbsp (15–30ml) oil as necessary.

Toast the coriander and cumin seeds in a dry skillet over medium heat for about a minute until fragrant. Using a mortar and pestle, grind the toasted spices, peppercorns, and salt to a fine powder. Tip this into the food processor and add the shrimp paste, if using. Blend until the mixture is well combined, stopping to scrape down the sides of the bowl a few times, to ensure an evenly ground wet paste.

To prepare the curry, slice the beef into bite-size pieces and set aside. Similarly, cut the eggplants into bite-size pieces and put to one side.

Heat the oil in a large pan or wok. Add 3–4 tbsp (45–60ml) of the curry paste and stir over medium heat until fragrant. Add the coconut milk and bring to a simmer. When the oil separates from the milk, add the eggplants, chiles, lime leaves, fish sauce, and sugar. Cook for 3 to 4 minutes until the eggplants are tender, then add the beef and cook for another 2 minutes. Remove the pan from the heat.

Ladle the curry into warm bowls and scatter over the basil or cilantro. Serve immediately, with steaming bowls of fragrant jasmine rice.

Stir-fried **chicken** with **cashews**

NUTS ARE OFTEN ADDED TO THAI STIR-FRIES, just as they are to similar Chinese dishes. The important thing to remember when stir-frying is to have all the ingredients prepared and the vegetables chopped before you fire up the wok. Once you start cooking, it literally takes minutes to get the dish to the table.

SERVES 4

2–3 boneless, skinless chicken breasts, about 14oz (400g) in total
sea salt and black pepper
2 tbsp (30ml) vegetable or peanut oil
1/3 cup (50g) cashews
1 small onion, peeled and sliced
3 garlic cloves, peeled and chopped
1 dried red chile, cut into 1/2-inch (1cm) pieces
3 green onions, trimmed and cut on the diagonal into 1 1/4-inch (3cm) pieces
4 tsp (20ml) fish sauce
1 tbsp (15ml) dark soy sauce
pinch of superfine sugar
1 red chile, seeded and sliced on the diagonal

Cut the chicken breasts into bite-size pieces and mix with a pinch each of salt and pepper. Set aside.

Heat the oil in a wok or a wide skillet. Add the cashews and stir over medium heat until toasted and lightly golden. Remove from the wok with a slotted spoon and set aside.

Add the onion and garlic to the wok and stir-fry for 3 to 4 minutes. Tip in the dried chile, then add the chicken pieces. Stir-fry for 2 minutes until the chicken is opaque. Add the green onions, fish sauce, soy sauce, and a pinch of sugar and stir-fry for another minute. Finally, tip in the sliced red chile and toasted cashews. Stir well and turn off the heat.

Spoon the mixture onto a warm platter or divide between warm bowls and serve immediately, with freshly steamed jasmine rice.

Spicy stir-fried vegetables

USE ANY COLORFUL COMBINATION of vegetables you fancy for this tasty dish. Just take care to avoid overcooking—the vegetables should be just tender but still retain a lovely crunch as you bite into them.

SERVES 4

1 large onion, peeled and sliced

1 medium carrot, peeled and sliced on the diagonal

2 garlic cloves, peeled and chopped

1¼-inch (3cm) piece of gingerroot, peeled and cut into sticks

3½oz (100g) shiitake mushrooms, cleaned and sliced

1 sweet red pepper, cored, seeded, and cut into strips

1 small head of broccoli, trimmed and cut into tiny florets

3 green onions, trimmed and cut into finger lengths

2 tbsp (30ml) vegetable or peanut oil

Sauce:

3 tbsp (45ml) vegetable or chicken stock

2 tbsp (30ml) fish sauce, or to taste

2 tbsp (30ml) light soy sauce

1 tbsp (15ml) lime juice, or to taste

1 tbsp (15ml) runny honey (or superfine sugar), or to taste

2 tsp (10ml) cornstarch, mixed with 3 tbsp (45ml) water

pinch of dried red pepper flakes

Have all the vegetables and aromatics prepared and ready to cook. In a bowl, mix together the ingredients for the sauce.

Place a wok or a wide skillet over medium heat. Add the oil and swirl it around the wok to coat. Add the onion and stir-fry for a minute. Add the carrot, garlic, and gingerroot and stir-fry for another minute. Now add the mushrooms and stir-fry for another couple of minutes until the carrot begins to soften.

Tip the red pepper, broccoli, and green onions into the wok, then pour over the sauce. Stir-fry for another 2 to 3 minutes until the pepper and broccoli have both softened slightly but still retain a bite. Taste and adjust the seasoning, adding a little more fish sauce, lime juice, or honey as needed.

Divide the stir-fry between warm plates or bowls and serve immediately.

Pad Thai with shrimp

ONE OF THE MOST POPULAR DISHES on Thai restaurant menus, this isn't difficult to make at home. You just need to make sure that you don't overcrowd the wok. So, if you decide to increase the quantities here—to serve more guests—cook the noodles in batches, two portions at a time.

SERVES 2

4oz (125g) thin or medium dried rice noodles
4 tsp (20ml) superfine sugar
2 tbsp (30ml) fish sauce
2 tbsp (30ml) tamarind paste (or lime juice)
4 tbsp (60ml) vegetable oil
1 shallot, peeled and chopped
2 large garlic cloves, peeled and chopped
$1/2$ red chile, seeded and minced
$3^{1}/_{2}$oz (100g) raw shrimp, peeled and deveined
2 medium eggs
generous $^{3}/_{4}$ cup (50g) bean sprouts
2 green onions, trimmed, green part only, cut into finger lengths
3 tbsp (45ml) roasted chopped peanuts, to sprinkle
lime wedges, to serve

Soak the rice noodles in boiling water for about 10 minutes until flexible and pliable but not overly soft, or cook according to the package instructions. (Some dried noodles need to be blanched in boiling water for several minutes to soften them.)

Meanwhile, combine the sugar, fish sauce, and tamarind paste in a small bowl and stir well. When ready, drain the noodles and set aside.

Heat half the oil in a wok or a large nonstick skillet until hot. Add the shallot, garlic, and chile and stir over medium heat until fragrant. Tip in the shrimp and stir-fry for a couple of minutes until they turn orangey pink and opaque. Remove the shrimp to a plate with a slotted spoon and set aside.

Drain the rice noodles and add to the wok with the sauce and a little splash of water. Stir-fry for a few minutes until they are tender. Push the ingredients in the wok to one side and add a little more oil to the other side. Crack the eggs over the oil and scramble lightly until they are almost cooked, then fold into the noodles.

Return the shrimp to the wok and add the bean sprouts and green onions. Stir briefly over the heat, until the vegetables are slightly wilted but still crunchy.

Divide the pad Thai between warm shallow serving bowls and sprinkle with the chopped peanuts. Serve immediately, with lime wedges.

Banana fritters
with **sesame** seeds

I LIKE TO EAT THESE SWEET HOT FRITTERS with a scoop of contrasting cold, creamy vanilla ice cream. Pure indulgence. You do need to eat them fairly soon after cooking to enjoy them at their crispy best.

SERVES 6–8

5–6 large, firm but ripe bananas
vegetable or peanut oil, for
   deep-frying
confectioners' sugar, to dust

Batter:
2 tbsp (30ml) desiccated coconut
3/4 cup (100g) rice flour
scant 1 cup (100g) cornstarch
4 tbsp (60ml) sesame seeds
1 tsp (5ml) fine sea salt
2 tbsp (30ml) superfine sugar
about 1 cup (250ml) water

First, prepare the batter. Put the desiccated coconut, rice flour, cornstarch, sesame seeds, salt, and sugar into a large bowl and stir well. Make a well in the center of the dry ingredients and pour in most of the the water. Stir until evenly blended and there are no lumps. The batter should be fairly thick, but add more water if it seems too dense.

About 10 minutes before you will be ready to serve, peel the bananas and cut each one into 3 or 4 short lengths. Heat a 2–2 1/2 inch (5–6cm) depth of oil in a wok or deep heavy saucepan until hot. To test if the oil is hot enough, drop a little batter into the pan—it should sizzle immediately.

Cook the fritters in batches. Dip the banana pieces in the batter to coat all over, then carefully lower them into the hot oil. Deep-fry for a few minutes until golden brown all over, turning once. Remove and drain on a plate lined with paper towels. Keep warm, while you cook the rest of the fritters.

Dust the crisp, hot banana fritters with confectioners' sugar and serve straightaway.

Mango, lime, and coconut rice pudding

A LOVELY FRAGRANT RICE PUDDING that can be served hot or chilled if you prefer. If you decide to chill it, hold off preparing and adding the mango until you are ready to serve.

SERVES 4–6

1¼ cups (250g) jasmine rice
14oz (400ml) can coconut milk
    (reduced-fat, if preferred)
scant ½ cup (80g) superfine sugar
1 vanilla bean, slit in half
    lengthwise
2–3 tbsp (30–45ml) desiccated
    coconut
1 ripe mango
⅔ cup (150ml) heavy cream

To serve:
handful of pistachios, chopped
1 lime, for zesting

Put the rice, coconut milk, sugar, and vanilla bean into a saucepan. Bring to a simmer, stirring frequently, then cover the pan and cook for about 15 to 20 minutes until the rice is tender.

Meanwhile, lightly toast the coconut in a dry skillet over medium heat until golden brown, shaking the pan frequently. Tip onto a plate and let cool. Peel the mango and cut the flesh into chunks, away from the seed.

When the rice is ready, remove the pan from the heat and remove the vanilla bean. Stir in the toasted coconut, heavy cream, and mango pieces until evenly combined. Cover again and allow to stand for 2 to 3 minutes.

Divide the rice pudding between serving bowls and scatter the chopped pistachios on top. Lightly grate over some lime zest and serve.

Carrot and coconut halwa

HALWAS VARY SIGNIFICANTLY IN TEXTURE. Some recipes produce a soft pudding, but I prefer to cook the mixture until it is sticky and thick enough to be rolled into balls, which I coat with toasted desiccated coconut. I also add some chopped pistachios and almonds to the carrot mixture for a slightly nutty texture. Serve with coffee, or as a dessert or coffee time treat.

MAKES 18–20

4lb (2kg) carrots, peeled
2 cups (500ml) evaporated milk
2^1/$_2$ cups (500g) granulated sugar
3^1/$_2$ tbsp (50ml) unsalted butter
2 cardamom pods, seeds extracted and finely crushed
scant ^{1}/$_4$ cup (25g) toasted pistachios, minced
scant ^{1}/$_4$ cup (25g) toasted almonds, minced
^{1}/$_2$ cup (50g) desiccated coconut, lightly toasted

Coarsely grate the carrots and put them into a large heavy saucepan with the evaporated milk and granulated sugar. Bring to a boil and then lower the heat to a simmer. Cook for 35 to 45 minutes, stirring frequently, until all the milk has evaporated and the carrot is quite dry.

Add the butter to the saucepan and increase the heat slightly to roast the grated carrots. Cook for another 25 to 30 minutes, stirring frequently, until the mixture is dry. When it leaves the sides of the pan clean, take off the heat and stir in the crushed cardamom seeds and minced nuts.

Transfer the mixture to a wide dish and let cool completely, then chill for at least an hour to allow it to firm up more.

With wet hands, roll the mixture into neat round balls, then roll each ball in the toasted coconut to coat all over. The halwa are now ready to serve. They can be kept in a sealed container in the refrigerator for up to a week.

AMERICAN

WELL WHAT CAN I SAY ABOUT AMERICAN FOOD? GUTSY
AND GENEROUS, IT'S NOT FOR THE FAINT-HEARTED,
BUT THAT'S NOT TO SAY THAT ALL AMERICAN FOOD IS
RICH AND HEAVY. I SPEND A LOT OF TIME IN LOS
ANGELES. WE HAVE A RESTAURANT IN THE CITY, AND
ANOTHER OVER IN NEW YORK. AS WITH MOST VAST
COUNTRIES, THE FOOD VARIES A LOT DEPENDING ON
WHERE YOU ARE. NEW YORK, FOR EXAMPLE, IS MUCH
MORE EUROPEAN IN ITS APPROACH TO COOKING
COMPARED TO OTHER STATES. I WOULD CERTAINLY
RECOMMEND THE BUFFALO CHICKEN WINGS—THEY ARE
FANTASTIC—AND THE DESSERTS ARE TO DIE FOR ...

Chicken pot pie

MUCH LIKE THE BRITISH VERSION but with a lighter sauce, this classic American pie is terrific winter comfort food. Traditionally, a whole chicken is poached until tender, then the poaching liquor is reduced to make a flavorful stock for the pie. My simplified, but no less delicious, version uses tender chicken breasts; alternatively you could use leftover chicken from a previous night's roast.

SERVES 4

3¹/₂ tbsp (50ml) butter

1 large onion, peeled and chopped

3 celery stalks, trimmed and diced

1 large carrot, peeled and chopped

1 large potato, peeled and diced

generous ¹/₃ cup (50g) all-purpose flour, plus extra to dust

2 cups (500ml) chicken stock

generous 1 cup (250ml) light cream

sea salt and black pepper

1lb (500g) skinless, boneless chicken breasts, cut into bite-size pieces

10oz (300g) good-quality ready-made all-butter puff pastry

1 medium egg mixed with 1 tbsp (15ml) water (egg wash), to glaze

Melt the butter in a large, wide pan and add the onion, celery, carrot, and potato. Sauté gently for 10 minutes or until the vegetables are soft. Add the flour and stir well. Cook, stirring frequently, for another 2 minutes to cook out the flour.

Pour in the stock and cream and season well with salt and pepper. Bring to a simmer and cook, stirring, for about 5 to 10 minutes until thickened. Add the chicken and simmer for 5 minutes or until the pieces are just cooked through. Taste and adjust the seasoning. Take the pan off the heat and let cool slightly.

Preheat the oven to 400°F (200°C). Spoon the chicken filling into one large or 4 individual pie dish(es) to fill to just below the rim(s). Roll out the puff pastry on a lightly floured counter to a large circle, ¹/₈ inch (3mm) thick. Cut out a circle (or 4 small ones) large enough to form pie lid(s).

Reroll the trimmings and cut long strips to fit around the rim of the dish(es). Brush the rim(s) with water, position the pastry strips, and brush these with egg wash. Lift the pastry lid on top and crimp the edges to seal. If you wish, decorate the top of the pie with leaves cut from the pastry trimmings. Brush the pastry with egg wash to glaze.

Bake the pie in the oven for 40 to 50 minutes or until the pastry is golden brown and the filling is bubbling hot. Let stand for a few minutes before serving.

Blue **cheese burgers**

THE ADDITION OF CRUMBLY BLUE CHEESE gives these homemade burgers a lovely savory edge. They take little time and effort to make and taste far superior to commercially made burgers. Baked sweet potato wedges and coleslaw (see page 243) are ideal accompaniments.

SERVES 6–8

Burgers:
2lb (1kg) lean ground beef
1 small red onion, peeled and
   minced
3^1/$_2$oz (100g) blue cheese,
   crumbled
small bunch of chives, chopped
few dashes of Tabasco sauce
2 tsp (10ml) Worcestershire sauce
1 tsp (5ml) English mustard
sea salt and black pepper
olive oil, to drizzle

To serve:
6–8 soft burger buns, split
handful of salad leaves
sliced tomatoes
sliced avocado
mayonnaise and/or tomato
   ketchup

To prepare the burgers, put all the ingredients, except the oil, into a large bowl, seasoning well with salt and pepper. Mix until well combined, using your hands. Break off a small piece of the mixture, shape into a ball, and cook in an oiled pan until cooked, then taste for seasoning. Adjust the seasoning of the uncooked mixture as necessary. Cover the bowl with plastic wrap and chill for a few hours.

Preheat a griddle pan or heat up the barbecue. With wet hands, shape the burgers into 6–8 neat patties. Brush or drizzle the patties with a little olive oil and cook for about 7 to 10 minutes, turning them over halfway through cooking. They should still be slightly pink in the center.

When the burgers are almost ready, drizzle the cut side of the burger buns with a little olive oil. Toast the buns, cut-side down, on the barbecue or griddle until lightly golden.

To serve, sandwich the burger patties between the buns with some salad leaves, tomato and avocado slices, and a dollop of mayonnaise and/or ketchup, as you prefer.

5 ways with steak

Classic **steak tartare**

Finely dice 14oz (400g) tenderloin steak. In a bowl, whisk 2 egg yolks with 1 tbsp (15ml) Worcestershire sauce and a pinch of cayenne pepper. Add the steak along with 2 minced gherkins, 1 chopped shallot, 1 tbsp (15ml) Dijon mustard, 2 minced anchovy fillets, and a handful of chopped Italian parsley. Season with sea salt and black pepper and mix well. Shape the beef into patties and serve on pumperknickel bread or with fries. SERVES 4

Skirt or flank **steak** with **chimichurri sauce**

For the sauce, mix 2 generous handfuls each of chopped cilantro and parsley with 1 crushed garlic clove, 1 tbsp (15ml) white wine vinegar, a squeeze of lemon juice, and generous 1/3 cup (100ml) olive oil. Score the surface of an 1 3/4 lb (800g) piece skirt or flank steak against the grain and cut into 4 pieces. Lay in a dish, spoon on a third of the sauce, and let marinate in the refrigerator for at least 2 hours, overnight if possible. Heat the broiler to maximum or set a griddle pan over high heat. Remove the steak from the marinade, brush off excess, and season both sides with sea salt and black pepper. Cook for 2 to 3 minutes each side. Serve the steaks topped with the remaining sauce. SERVES 4

Peppered **steak** with **truffle** creamed **mushrooms**

Heat 1 tbsp (15ml) olive oil in a pan and gently sauté 1 minced onion and 1 minced garlic clove until softened but not colored. Add another 1 tbsp (15ml) oil, a piece of butter, and 2 2/3 cups (200g) sliced mixed mushrooms and cook until browned. Pour in 1/4 cup (50ml) white wine and let bubble until quite dry. Add 1 tsp (5ml) truffle oil, 1 tsp (5ml) minced black truffle if available, and 1 1/4 cups (300ml) heavy cream. Let simmer while you cook the steaks. Crush 1 1/2 tbsp (40ml) black peppercorns and scatter on a plate. Season four 8oz (250g) boneless rib eye steaks all over with sea salt, then press both sides into the crushed peppercorns. Place a heavy skillet over high heat and add 2 tbsp (30ml) olive oil. When the skillet is really hot, cook the steaks for 3 minutes on each side. The steaks should feel slightly springy for medium rare. Rest for a few minutes before serving, with the truffle creamed mushrooms. SERVES 4

Sirloin **steak** with **beer** and **onion** gravy

Season 4 sirloin steaks, about 8oz (250g) each, on both sides with sea salt and black pepper. Melt 4 tsp (20ml) butter in a large skillet over medium heat. When the skillet is really hot, add the steaks and cook for 3 to 4 minutes on each side for medium rare. Transfer to a warm plate, cover with foil, and keep warm in a low oven while you make the gravy. Add another piece of butter to the skillet along with 3 finely sliced onions and 2 tsp (10ml) superfine sugar. Cook over medium-high heat until golden brown and caramelized. Add 1 tsp (5ml) flour and cook for 1 minute, then stir in 3/4 cup (200ml) beer and 1 1/4 cups (300ml) beef stock. Let bubble for 8 to 10 minutes until thickened. Place each steak on a warm plate and spoon over the beer and onion gravy. SERVES 4

Chargrilled **steak** with **tomato** and **herb butter**

For the butter, blend scant 1 cup (100g) drained sun-dried tomatoes, 1 chopped garlic clove, and 1 chopped shallot in a food processor until smooth. Add 2/3 cup (150g) softened unsalted butter and a handful of chopped Italian parsley and chives. Blend again briefly, then scrape out onto a piece of plastic wrap and roll tightly in the wrap to form a cylinder, 1 1/4 inches (3cm) in diameter. Chill until ready to serve. Place a griddle pan over high heat until smoking hot. Brush 4 sirloin steaks, about 8–10oz (250–300g) each, with olive oil and season on both sides with sea salt and black pepper. Griddle for 3 minutes on each side for medium rare. Transfer to warm plates and let rest for a few minutes. Top each steak with a couple of slices of herb butter to serve. SERVES 4

Barbecued short ribs
with coleslaw

BARBECUED RIBS ARE A GREAT CHOICE if you are feeding a crowd. I slow-cook them in a flavorful braising liquor beforehand so that they only need a few minutes on the barbecue. The rich, sticky barbecue glaze imparts a superb flavor. Of course, you can easily scale down the recipe to serve 4, 6, or 8.

SERVES 12

6 racks of pork spareribs, each
    with 6–7 ribs
3 tbsp (45ml) tomato paste
2 onions, peeled and quartered
4 garlic cloves, lightly smashed
3/4 tsp (4ml) black peppercorns
5 cloves
2 dried red chiles
sea salt and black pepper

For the barbecue glaze:
4 tbsp (60ml) dark molasses
2 onions, peeled and minced
4 tbsp (60ml) runny honey
4 tbsp (60ml) Worcestershire
    sauce
2 tbsp (30ml) tomato paste
2 tbsp (30ml) English mustard
2 tbsp (30ml) cider vinegar
few good dashes of Tabasco sauce
juice of 1 lemon

Coleslaw:
1 small white cabbage, trimmed
4 large carrots, peeled and grated
1/2 cup (125ml) mayonnaise
4 tbsp (60ml) grainy mustard
2 tbsp (30ml) lemon juice
2–3 tsp (10–15ml) superfine sugar

First, braise the ribs—you'll need a saucepan in which they will fit snugly (divide each rack in half if it's easier). Pour about 8 cups (2 liters) water into the pan and add the tomato paste, onions, garlic, peppercorns, cloves, and dried chiles. Bring to a boil and let it bubble rapidly for 15 minutes. Add the rib racks and some seasoning. Top off with more water as necessary to ensure the ribs are covered and bring back to a gentle simmer. Skim off any scum or froth from the surface of the liquid. Simmer for about 45 to 60 minutes until the meat on the ribs is tender, adding more water during cooking if it reduces too much. Remove the pan from the heat and set aside to cool.

For the glaze, strain the braising liquor through a fine strainer into another pan and boil steadily until reduced by two-thirds. Add the molasses, onions, honey, Worcestershire sauce, tomato paste, mustard, cider vinegar, Tabasco, lemon juice, and salt and pepper. Stir over high heat for 6 to 8 minutes, until the mixture begins to bubble and is syrupy.

For the coleslaw, finely shred the white cabbage and toss in a large bowl with the grated carrots. For the dressing, mix the mayonnaise, mustard, lemon juice, and superfine sugar together, then add to the cabbage mix. Toss well and season with salt and pepper to taste. Cover and chill until ready to serve.

Prepare the barbecue and let the fire burn down to gray embers. Alternatively, preheat a griddle pan until hot.

When ready to serve, brush the glaze liberally over the ribs then barbecue or griddle for 1 1/2 to 2 minutes on each side (also illustrated overleaf). Serve with the coleslaw and crusty bread.

Project director Anne Furniss
Creative director Helen Lewis
Project editors Janet Illsley, Kathy Steer
Photographer Chris Terry
Food stylist Mark Sargeant
Home economist Emily Quah, assisted by Emily Shardlow
Props stylist Cynthia Inions
Designer Katherine Case
Production Vincent Smith, Ruth Deary

Optomen Television:
Managing director Pat Llewellyn
F Word executive producers
Jon Swain and Ben Adler
Series editor Jenny Crowther
'Head of potatoes' Sarah Durdin Robertson

Optomen Television Limited
1, Valentine Place
London SE1 8QH

www.optomen.com
First published in 2010 by Quadrille Publishing Limited
Alhambra House, 27-31 Charing Cross Road, London WC2H 0LS
www.quadrille.co.uk

Text © 2010 Gordon Ramsay
Photography © 2010 Chris Terry
Design and layout © 2010 Quadrille Publishing Limited
Format and programme © 2009 Optomen Television Limited

Library and Archives Canada Cataloguing in Publication
Ramsay, Gordon
    Gordon Ramsay's world kitchen : recipes from the F-word.
ISBN 978-1-55470-199-5
    1. Cookery, International. I. Title. II. Title: World kitchen.
TX725.A1R34 2010   641.59   C2010-901882-6

ONTARIO ARTS COUNCIL
CONSEIL DES ARTS DE L'ONTARIO

The publisher gratefully acknowledges the support of the Canada Council for the Arts and the Ontario Arts Council for its publishing program. We acknowledge the support of the Government of Ontario through the Ontario Media Development Corporation's Ontario Book Initiative.

We acknowledge the financial support of the Government of Canada through the Book Publishing Industry Development Program (BPIDP) for our publishing activities.

Key Porter Books Limited
Six Adelaide Street East, Tenth Floor
Toronto, Ontario
Canada M5C 1H6
www.keyporter.com
Printed and bound in China

10 11 12 13 14 6 5 4 3 2 1